HAUNTED
BUTLER COUNTY,
OHIO

HAUNTED
BUTLER COUNTY, OHIO

DANIEL D. SCHNEIDER

Haunted
America

Published by Haunted America
A Division of The History Press
Charleston, SC
www.historypress.com

Front cover: The Butler County Soldiers, Sailors and Pioneers Monument. *Author's collection.*

First published 2023

Manufactured in the United States

ISBN 9781467152556

Library of Congress Control Number: 2023934798

Notice: The information in this book is true and complete to the best of our knowledge. It is offered without guarantee on the part of the author or The History Press. The author and The History Press disclaim all liability in connection with the use of this book.

This book is dedicated to my sister, Dee Schneider, because when I was sick once, she rode her bike, uphill both ways in the rain and/or snow, to get me a couple bottles of Gatorade. It's been thirty-six years, and she still reminds me.

It's also dedicated to Shelly Harrison, because after many beers one night, she asked if I would.
Apparently, I said yes.

CONTENTS

Acknowledgements

Thanks to Mom and Dad; Dave and Debbie Schneider; my sister, Dee; and my buddies Matt Munafo and Jason Allen. Rick Fornshell and Butch Frederick at the Monument. Brad Spurlock and the staff of the Lane Public Library, the Butler County Historical Society, MidPoint Library and Miami University Library. Judy Shillinglaw, Jim Price and Scott Fowler at the Monroe Historical Society. The folks at the Sorg Opera House and Mica Glaser-Jones from the Windamere. Chris Rogers from the Hamilton Ghost Stories Facebook page, an excellent resource that was started by his father, Sam Rogers. Jana Harmon and the Fiehrer family for their Venice Pavilion stories. Heidi Schiller and the Fairfield Historical Society. Pat and Tasha Cain, former owners of the Hitching Post and new owners Britt Colson and Evan Cusmano and Evan's mom, Lisa. Fred Lindley for keeping Darrtown's history alive in the digital age. Matt Pater from the Arches. Darrell Whisman and his team at the Poasttown Elementary School. Laura and Jim Goodman for the great stories from Municipal Brew Works. Frank Munafo for his dorm ghost story. John Rodrigue at The History Press for making it happen! And finally, a big thanks to anyone I forgot to mention.

If you have any haunted or strange Butler County stories, please visit https://www.facebook.com/HauntedButlerCountyOhio or email HauntedButlerCountyOhio@gmail.com.

Introduction

History Through Hauntings

It was a dark and stormy night… Actually, it was so long ago, and I don't know if it was dark and stormy or not, but I always wanted to start a book like that. The beginning of this book came about many decades ago. It was a term paper for a class at Badin High School. I gathered all the local ghost stories and even made hand-drawn maps. I never thought it would become a book years later.

People may ask, "What do ghost stories have to do with history?" They are a direct link to yesteryear. They are the folklore of the region. They also tie the reader back to the social history of the area at a specific time. The stories are about people, places and events from a distinct era. If someone says they are going to give a history lesson, most wouldn't really be interested. If someone says they have a ghost story to tell, it catches their attention. To understand a ghost story, one must first learn the history to find out "why" it is haunted. The more I researched, the more things came to light. Some stories that were lost were found; some stories that people believed were known, weren't. Throughout this book, I tell the history of the people, places and things from Butler County's long and sometimes gruesome past. They are what give the details and validity to support the ghost stories. Most of the stories seem to have a basis in fact. The who, what, when or where may have changed and evolved over decades in the stories, but if you dig deep enough, frequently you can find the "why" behind the hauntings.

MY HOUSE

I purchased a historic home in Hamilton in early 2020. The problem with an old home is leaks, especially if it has a flat roof. So repair work began. During the work, I noticed tools coming up missing, Phillips head screwdrivers and tape measures being the most common. They would show up in places I knew I had looked, places that would have been obvious, like the center of a counter or table. The disappearing and reappearing tools caught my attention because of the man who built the house.

John Spoerl worked in the hardware business for seventy-four years, beginning in 1873, getting his start at the age of fourteen in downtown Hamilton working at the Davidson and Schliep Hardware Store. On their passing, he purchased their shares, becoming the full owner. When Spoerl passed away at eighty-eight in February 1947, he was the oldest hardware merchant in Ohio. It seems appropriate that my tools randomly disappear and reappear.

Other strange things have happened in the house. There are mysterious crashes, where a search of the house reveals nothing has fallen over. It sounds like a bunch of boxes falling. I always try to find a reasonable explanation for any occurrence. I'll hear footsteps, which I attribute to the house settling, pipes rattling or an unusually fat squirrel walking on the roof. Recently, I had the footsteps approach my bed at night. I just tell myself that it was definitely a squirrel. I have seen shadows cast on walls; those I assume were from car headlights, even if I didn't see a car. The voices I occasionally hear I think probably came from outside, even though with the thick walls of the house, you can't really even hear the Pleasant Avenue traffic. One day, I heard coughing from behind me as I was at my computer working; I think that was a previous owner. One event I have not been able to explain was when I had a pizza on the counter and walked out of the room; when I walked back in, I saw the lid open and fall back against the counter ledge. Maybe my ghosts also crave the local favorite, Chester's Pizza?

CHAPTER 1
NATIVE SPIRITS

Archaeologists believe humans have been in Ohio for around fourteen thousand years. They left behind mounds and earthworks, many of which have been lost to time. These mounds and earthworks were built by the Adena and Hopewell cultures. Most of these works have been lost due to farming, erosion and development. Many were surveyed and descriptions written before they were completely wiped from existence. Many books were written on them, including William Mills's *Archeological Atlas of Ohio*, which states that in 1914, there were 221 mounds and 30 earthworks still located in Butler County.

THE ANCIENT ONES OF REILY

Chris Rogers, an avid outdoorsman and hunter, had a hard-to-explain experience while hunting in the woods north of Reily. In the early '90s, Chris obtained permission to hunt a tract of land that backed up to Indian Creek. During his second year hunting there, he experienced a truly terrifying incident. On a dark, moonless morning around four o'clock, he walked into the woods toward his tree stand, using his flashlight. As he approached the tree line, he turned off the light, letting his eyes adjust to the darkness. He listened for any telltale sounds of deer or anything in the vicinity. Occasionally he might catch the sound of an owl or coyote; this night, he

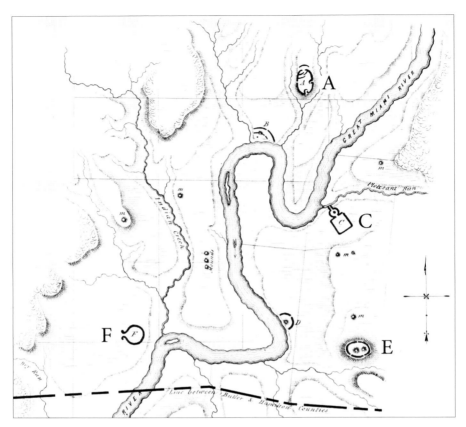

Map by J.W. Erwin showing the Great Miami River Valley south of Hamilton with the ancient mounds and earthworks, from Squier and Davis's *Ancient Monuments of the Mississippi Valley*. *Author's collection.*

heard a sound like the beating of wings. He realized it was too rhythmic and lasting too long to be wild turkeys—plus, it seemed to be getting louder. Suddenly, he noticed an eerie red glow in the woods. He realized the beating sounded more drumlike as the glow continued to brighten to the point where it seemed the entire top of the hill was glowing in the red light. The wind kicked up, but strangely, it only seemed to be blowing in the area of the glow, sending leaves flying through the air as the drumbeats continued to get louder. The red glow was casting shadows through the trees that looked like dark arms reaching toward him. The black shadow reached closer and closer...and then, in an instant, everything stopped. No light, no wind, no beating of drums; the only sound was Chris's heart pounding in his chest as he wondered what had just happened. The entire experience lasted maybe a minute. Chris didn't move from his spot for over a half an hour and never saw anyone leave the woods. Finally, he decided to walk into the woods to his tree stand, and about ten steps in, he heard the bloodcurdling scream of a hawk. He decided that he had had enough; he'd come back during the day. As he turned to leave, he felt an extremely uneasy feeling having his back to those woods. There was a woodpile nearby, and he sat with his back against it, so he could keep an eye on the tree line. He waited until sunrise, then decided to go back into the woods to see if there were any remnants of whatever he saw and heard. The only thing he noticed was the leaves that had been scattered around by the strange vortex of wind on the hill. He mentioned what happened to the owner of the land. The owner reluctantly said he had seen things in the woods also, and the hilltop was an Indian burial ground. The owner didn't have much else to say about it, and Chris didn't press the matter. He continued to come back to hunt the area many times after that incident and never experienced anything else. Reily Township has many Native American mounds and burial sites and two known earthworks stretched along Indian Creek. This must have been an important place for the ancient ones.

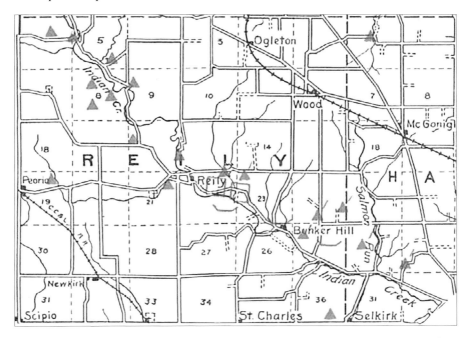

A portion of William C. Mills's 1914 Butler County map showing the native sites around Reily Township. *Author's collection.*

Rick Fornshell and his buddy Bill were out cruising the country roads of Reily Township, many years ago. As they were talking, Bill, who has Native ancestry, mentioned that it is not a good idea to walk into a certain part of the woods. He said it is sacred land and "they" don't want them there. Rick convinced Bill that they had to see for themselves. They hopped a fence and had journeyed about fifty yards when Bill pointed out a large depression in the ground and said, "That is not a good place; we are not going that way." They continued in another direction and came upon a large tree with a cavity underneath; the roots formed what looked like a cage. The depression was large enough that someone could lie underneath. Bill believed it was a place a shaman would use to connect to the forest. Suddenly, a crow landed on Bill's shoulder. The crow let out a loud caw and flew away. "It's time to leave," Bill said. They got up and began walking back the way they came. They walked and walked. They knew they came less than one hundred yards into the woods and walked a lot farther on the way out. They couldn't find the edge of the tree line or the fence! Rick said, "We are out in the woods all the time; we never get lost!" Bill replied, "We need to say we are sorry and promise to never come back into these woods again." Rick agreed, and they said to the spirits of the woods that they were just curious, that their curiosity had been satisfied and they would not return. As soon as they said this, they turned and saw the clearing from where they had started their journey.

The Ceremony

Years ago, three teens were in a farm field where they liked to search for relics. There were some great finds over the years: flint knives, arrowheads of high quality, banded slate banner stones and other items. One evening as darkness fell, something in the tree line separating the farm field from neighboring Joyce Park caught one of the teens' eye. It was a large bluish-green light that appeared to be moving closer, unwavering in its approach. Unsure what it was, they left—later realizing that they had walked that field many times and it is not the easiest to traverse in the daylight without slipping or falling. It had become night, and the light seemed to be steadily moving toward them. They always assumed there was a village in that area. Years later, one saw a large image of the Great Miami River Valley earthworks at the Ohio History Connection in Columbus. One of the earthworks

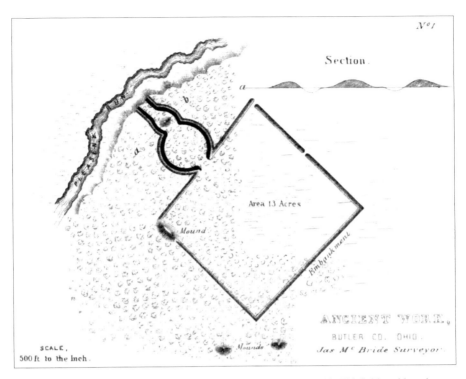

James McBride's survey of an earthwork structure that was located in Fairfield and has since been plowed and built over. It was located in the area near Water Works Park. *Author's collection.*

was in the field they used to frequent. It was a large square and circle with embankments leading to Pleasant Run Creek. Although the earthwork was plowed over decades ago, the path of the light would have been traveling directly toward that structure's former location. Now the area is farm fields, subdivisions, sports fields and possibly a pathway for ancient spirits repeating a lost ceremony.

SPIRIT OF THE MYAAMIA

The cornerstone of Miami University's first women's dormitory was laid in November 1904. It was named for then vice president of the university Andrew D. Hepburn. Hepburn Hall was dedicated in a grand ceremony in June 1905. Tragedy struck only a few years later in 1908, as flames erupted

Inside Hepburn Hall, 1905. *Miami University Archives, Frank R. Snyder Collection.*

Hepburn Hall after the 1908 fire. *Miami University Archives, Frank R. Snyder Collection.*

in the 150-room dormitory. Although the fire left one hundred young women homeless and without their belongings, there were no deaths. The walls were undamaged, and the building was reconstructed within the shell of the structure. The fire was determined to have been caused by wiring on the third floor. It was believed to have been smoldering in the insulation for a couple days, as some girls reported smelling wood burning and others reported their lights weren't working that day.

It's not known when the ghost was first seen, but on the third floor of the building, women began seeing a Native American man. No one knew who he was or why he was there. It was speculated that he had died on the land when the Miami tribes lived in the area. After the Treaty of Greenville, the Miami—or, as they referred to themselves, the Myaamia—were forced to give up land and moved further west little by little. By the 1830s, they had been reduced to five hundred thousand acres in Indiana. In 1840 they agreed to move, within five years, to an equivalently sized area in the Kansas Territory. In late 1846, about 325 remaining Myaamia were forcefully transported on the Wabash-Erie Canal from Peru, Indiana, to Fort Wayne, Indiana, then made their way to the Miami-Erie Canal, where they passed for their final time through Butler County on the way to Cincinnati and to the Ohio River. From Cincinnati, they made their way by steamboat to the Mississippi River, then to the Missouri River and finally, on November 5, 1846, to Kansas—only to ultimately be told that they would need to move again to the Oklahoma Territories.

The Miami tribe left their mark on the area. They left their name on the Great Miami and Little Miami Rivers, and the university that formed on part of their ancestral lands eventually came to bear their name. The fire in Hepburn Hall started on the third floor, the same floor that the Native spirit was seen. Maybe in life he refused to leave his native land and in death stayed to watch over it and the Miami University students. Hepburn Hall stopped being a dormitory in 1961 and eventually became Clokey Hall in 1964. It was demolished in 1965 to make way for the new King Library building, which opened in 1966. The name of Hepburn Hall was transferred to a new residence hall building that opened on another part of campus in 1964. It's not known if the spirit of the Miami tribe member moved to the new Hepburn Hall or if he now lingers around the library.

Spirits of the Woods

Hueston Woods State Park is a nearly three-thousand-acre state park located in both Butler and Preble Counties. It also contains some haunted locations. There is an Adena mound at the west end of the campground. The mound is very close to a trailhead. This mound has been the subject of many photographs over the years. Sometimes people have caught things in the photos that they can't explain: a blur or a figure in the background or points of light that were not seen when the photo was taken.

In the fall of 1792, Miami chief Little Turtle and more than two hundred of his men planned to attack Fort Washington. While en route, they captured two soldiers east of Fort Hamilton and learned of a large supply train. Little Turtle changed his plan and decided to intercept the supply train and take the horses. On the night of November 6, Little Turtle and his men found the wagon train camped outside Fort St. Clair. In the ensuing battle, six soldiers were killed, the camp was plundered and the survivors managed to retreat inside the fort. According to local legends, a soldier haunts the site of Fort St. Clair in Eaton, and people have seen flickering lights at night among the trees around Hueston Woods and believe these are the torches of Little Turtle and his men.

The Adena mound is located in Hueston Woods, where strange anomalies have been captured on camera. *Author's collection.*

CHAPTER 2
PIONEER POLTERGEISTS

MONUMENTAL GHOSTS

On July 20, 1897, the Grand Army of the Republic's Wetzel-Compton Post 96 formed a plan to commemorate the gallantry of the Butler County men who served in the armed forces and people who settled this frontier. First, they needed a suitable location. On January 18, 1898, the Hamilton city council passed an ordinance giving land to the committee. The location was very fitting: it was where Fort Hamilton had stood. The cornerstone was laid on Thanksgiving Day 1902 following a parade with many Civil War and Spanish-American War veterans in attendance.

The final structure is an admirable one-hundred-foot-tall neoclassical building with steel framework clad in sandstone. The interior walls are covered with the names of pioneers and Butler County veterans through the Spanish-American War. The second floor has beautiful art glass windows depicting women's contributions to the war efforts. Above the second floor is a colonnade with a cupola, and on top of that stands the seventeen-foot-tall bronze statue created by local artist Rudolph Thiem. The seventeen-foot, 3,500-pound sculpture of a Civil War Union soldier is seen holding a musket in his right hand and holding his hat aloft in his left as he celebrates the end of the war. The sculpture's named *Victory, the Jewel of the Soul* but is known by locals as Billy Yank. There is one story that grandpas love to tell their grandsons and probably have every year since

The impressive Soldiers, Sailors and Pioneers Monument stands proudly over the edge of the Great Miami River. *Author's collection.*

the statue was set in place. During the day, Billy Yank faces east looking down High Street, but at night, when no one is looking, he turns to face the Great Miami River to relieve himself.

The early days of Fort Hamilton were not easy. The fort was built by hand with an inadequate supply of substandard tools. The forest was so thick that the men themselves had to carry the fifteen- to twenty-foot logs instead of using carts and livestock to haul them. The entire operation was also done with great speed. It only took two weeks and one hundred men to build the fort. It was given the name of Fort Hamilton, in honor of Alexander Hamilton, after construction was completed on September 30, 1791.

Desertions on the frontier were not an unusual occurrence. Many of the men were militiamen who signed on for six-month tours on the frontier and were not trained soldiers. The most notorious story is about seven deserters from 1793, three of whom were hanged, including one who may remain.

As a volunteer, Rick Fornshell spends a lot of time in the basement of the Butler County Soldiers, Sailors and Pioneers Monument—or just the Monument—cataloguing and archiving pieces of Butler County history. One time, a medium visited the building and described feeling a disturbed soul in the basement of the monument. Rick wondered who or what it could have been. Shortly thereafter, another worker at the monument told him about a hanging of some court-martialed deserters that didn't end well. This spurred some ideas, and Rick had a feeling this story could be related to the spirit in the basement.

Major Michael Rudolph and his group of men arrived at Fort Hamilton in the fall of 1792. Rudolph was to take command of the fort in 1793. In February, he was appointed inspector general of the army. A veteran of the Revolutionary War, Rudolph was also known as a very authoritarian officer. His men came from the more cosmopolitan areas back East and were not prepared for the wilderness of the Ohio frontier. Many were not happy to be there. In March, seven men escaped the confines of the fort and made their way south to the Ohio River. Once at the river, they obtained a canoe and began to make their way to New Orleans. Near Louisville, Lieutenant George Rogers Clark captured and arrested the deserters. He sent them back to Fort Hamilton under guard. Major Rudolph decided he must set an example to other potential deserters. *The Centennial History of Butler County* states a court-martial was ordered and that four of the men were sentenced to heavy punishments and three to hang the next day. Those three were John Brown, Seth Blinn and a man named Gallagher. A friend of the men, knowing the penalty for leaving the fort without permission, decided

Left: The sculpture that stands atop the monument building is affectionately called Billy Yank by locals but is officially named *Victory, the Jewel of the Soul. Author's collection.*

Below: Sketch of what Fort Hamilton may have looked like. *Lane Public Library Digital Collection.*

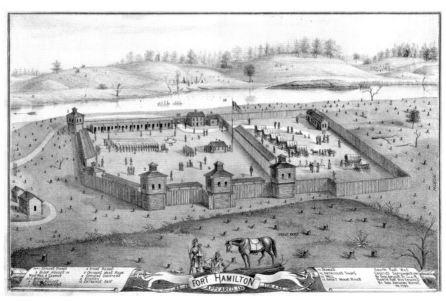

to ride to Fort Washington to plea with General Wilkinson, Rudolph's superior. Wilkinson granted the pardons, and the horseman fled back to Fort Hamilton, arriving fifteen minutes too late. John Brown had been the first to be hanged, and his final words were, "I would rather die nine deaths than be under the command of Rudolph!"

Seth Blinn joined the army because he was not allowed to marry a girl considered "beneath him." It was said that his was not a "clean" hanging. It was not an instant neck snap as it should have been. He jerked spasmodically, so hard that his feet were hitting his head. In April, General Anthony Wayne visited Fort Hamilton. On hearing about this event and its outcome, he became furious. This is not how a fort should be run, especially not by an inspector general of the United States Army. Wayne offered Rudolph two choices: resign or be cashiered, a disgraceful dismissal. Rudolph chose resignation. Rudolph's legend persisted afterward. Some say he fled to France to fight in the French Revolution; others say he died at the hands of pirates, hanged from his own yardarm. When Rick told the spirit that it was believed Rudolph was hanged, he said the mood seemed to lift in the basement.

Maintaining a monument of this importance is a daunting task. Guiding tours, creating exhibits and archiving historical relics are a daily part of the job. There have been many curators and volunteers in and out of these hallowed halls. One may have enjoyed her job so much that she hasn't left. Rick Fornshell says there have been times when he has been trying to locate things and has felt like someone was guiding him to the right locations. After a group did a paranormal investigation of the building, he decided to try one of their techniques to confirm his idea about who the spirit might be: using a twist-type flashlight, twisted to the point where it almost turns on. Theoretically, the spirit completes the circuit to make the light turn on and off as a means to answer questions. He believed it was the former curator, Ann Warren, and when he asked, the light immediately came on. He asked her to turn it off, and it blinked out on command. Ann was the curator for twenty-two years until her passing in April 1987. Ann was a veteran herself, having served in the Women's Army Auxiliary Corps from 1942 to 1944 during World War II. She loved being involved with planning parades, placing flags at cemeteries and other patriotic events in Butler County. Rick found a plaque of hers one day in storage, and it's now displayed in the south vestibule on the second floor.

Rick also mentioned a visit by the daughter of another former curator who was in town and stopped by to visit and reminisce about the days she

The donated German WWI helmet that may have a spiritual attachment to the soldier who wore it. *Author's collection.*

had spent there with her father. She happened to mention that she would sometimes go down to the basement to take naps. Her dad always told her, "Don't worry about anything you might hear; it's all good." That trend of strange sounds continues today. When the current curator—and veteran— Butch Frederick was asked if he had experienced anything, he said that he really hadn't but he keeps the patriotic music playing while he's there, just so he won't hear anything out of the ordinary!

There are also many artifacts, some on permanent display and some stored in the basement, archived so they can be retrieved for various rotating themed displays. One of these items that is currently in storage is a World War I German helmet. The black helmet has two notable holes in the back from pieces of shrapnel. That shrapnel would have killed anyone wearing the helmet. Rick tells about having a feeling of something in the basement that he believed was associated with the helmet. He would get the feeling of someone saying the name "Klaus"—not audibly—when he was near or handling the helmet. It seems the spirit has an attachment to the helmet that he was wearing while he was killed during the Great War.

THE GHOSTS OF COURTHOUSE SQUARE

The first Butler County Courthouse opened in 1817. Prior to that, proceedings took place at a building in the fort or a local tavern. The county was outgrowing the building by 1836, and it was remodeled multiple times until it was torn down in 1888 and replaced with the current courthouse building.

It's known among paranormal circles that when there is construction or renovations done, it seems to "stir up" something. It seemed to trigger a lot of activity in the 1890s when the previous courthouse structure was torn down and the new Butler County Courthouse was built. That could explain why former Butler County treasury clerk Matthew Hueston returned.

The headline in the January 5, 1893 *Middletown Signal* read:

> *A GHOST.*
> *That Haunts the Butler County Courthouse and Is Frightening the People of Hamilton.*

In late 1892, the courthouse janitor, George Bisdorf, noticed the clock in the treasury office had stopped. He reset it and thought nothing more of it. About a month later, night watchman Gary Longfellow was doing

The Butler County Courthouse, which had a ghostly visit by a former employee shortly after it opened its doors. *Author's collection.*

his rounds at midnight and heard the treasury office clock start its twelve gongs at midnight. He counted them off in his head: eleven, twelve, thirteen, fourteen, fifteen… The clock kept continuing. He went into the office, and the strikes of the clock seemed to get shriller with each strike of the bell, almost humanlike screams, then they stopped after twenty-one strikes. Puzzled, he turned to leave, then heard something coming from the clock behind him. He looked and saw a face forming; he recognized it as Matthew Hueston. He had a sad look on his face; he seemed as if he wanted to speak but couldn't. This wasn't the only time Matthew Hueston was seen. He is also said to have been seen and recognized at least once walking the grounds outside the courthouse between the hours of midnight and one o'clock, not looking ghostly but as if he were a normal man in normal clothing.

Who was Matthew Hueston? According to a June 1868 *Cincinnati Enquirer* article, a reporter visited the treasurer's office and met the treasurer-elect, John C. Lindley, and the current treasurer, David Brant, and

> *was pleased to form the acquaintance of Matthew Huston* [sic], *who, for years, has been connected with the office as a courteous and efficient clerk, and I doubt not that the day will come when the people will gladly give him the keys of the whole establishment.*

This was a prophetic choice of words: within a year Hueston had the keys to the whole establishment. He had clerked in the treasurer's office for many years, been an assistant to the treasurer and was also the night watchman—that is, until the morning of May 23, 1869, when he was found swinging by his neck from the chandelier in the vault. It was ruled a suicide. That wasn't the only death that morning. The former treasurer, David Bryant, also died unexpectedly. The May 25, 1869 *Cincinnati Enquirer* reported that Bryant was in Cincinnati on the twenty-second and was seen "in the enjoyment of robust and vigorous health," at least until he got home. Later that evening, he was experiencing chills and fever, and by one o'clock in the morning, was dead. A few months later, in February 1870, another shocking event happened: it was found that funds in the Butler County Treasury were being misused. Reportedly, $100,000 to $130,000 was declared to be missing, nearly $3 million today. Treasurer John C. Lindley had been taking money from the vault and loaning it. In February 1871, he faced trial for embezzlement. The suits against Lindley were dismissed in March 1872.

People were not happy with the dismissal, and many thought the corruption may have gone deeper. The December 3, 1873 *Cincinnati Enquirer* had the following headline:

A MYSTERY
Something for Hamilton People to Consider.
Was Matthew Huston [sic] *Murdered, or Did He Commit Suicide.*

An unknown informant believed Hueston was murdered, because he left no suicide note or will. He had received a $5,000 repayment earlier that day, and it was missing and not deposited. Also, two men were seen leaving the office around midnight. One was seen with a lot of cash shortly after. People wondered if the two men were there to steal the $5,000 or because Hueston "had secrets which might be dangerous to the ring," seemingly implying he was killed to protect the embezzlement ring. The *Enquirer*'s unknown informant posed a theory that these men were there to coerce Hueston into falsifying documents and put all the blame on former treasurer David Brant, who coincidentally died that same night. They continued to theorize that the men may have believed Hueston planned to expose them and decided to silence him forever—or so they thought.

An article in the *Eaton Register* went straight to the point, saying Lindley may have been responsible for the deaths of Hueston and Brant and that Lindley's "irregularities" began after the deaths of the two men. Lindley's fortunes also took a severe downturn over the next few years. He was indicted for obtaining money under false pretenses in Arkansas. In July 1874, Lindley was in Hamilton to meet with commissioners, hoping to see them bring suit against men he claimed were more guilty than himself. In 1877, Lindley was running a grocery and dry goods store in Reily. On February 26, 1877, a fire started in the building. As the fire spread, someone in the crowd yelled that there was gunpowder in the store. The crowd immediately moved away just as an explosion shook the town, destroying the building. In September 1878, the suit against Lindley and his bondsmen was finally abandoned, but karma—or something—wasn't finished with him. On December 12, 1878, John C. Lindley died from burns when a coal oil lamp exploded as he lit his morning fire in his kitchen.

The original 1893 *Middletown Signal* article mentioned that besides Hueston, many apparitions had been seen in and around the courthouse. Who could these spirits be? When Israel Ludlow laid out the plat for Hamilton, he set aside a square to be used for a courthouse and placed a cemetery at the edge of town. The early fort and pioneer burial grounds were near today's Front and High Streets, near the designated square, and those bodies were to be moved to the new cemetery. Except the old cemetery wasn't organized well, according to Anna Owens in her June 14, 1929 *Journal News* Early Hamilton column. Owens describes the land as it appeared in 1807:

> At that time nearly all east of Front Street was an impenetrable thicket…a thicket that it was only in some parts a man could make his way through them. True it is, paths and roads were in some places cut through them to admit of a free passage…and where the courthouse now is, the brushwood was very thick, although this space had been occupied as the garrison burying ground. The gravestones and graves were discoverable all over the tract of ground.

Which makes one wonder if all the bodies were moved.

SCALPED!

Even though peace was brokered with the Native Americans with the signing of the Treaty of Greenville in 1795, there were some tribes and individuals that were not fond of it. Zechariah DeWitt and his family built a log cabin along Four-Mile Creek in 1805. One day, his young wife, Elizabeth, was out picking blackberries when she noticed a Shawnee brave watching her, and she fled in panic. The brave gave chase; he knew he was not allowed to kill or kidnap the woman due to the treaty, yet he still desired a hunting trophy. He caught up to the woman and dragged her down by her long hair, the perfect trophy. He pulled out his hunting knife and ran it in a circle around her head, then tore off the bloody scalp and ran off into the woods. Elizabeth made it to her home, covered in blood. She told her husband what had happened, and Zechariah called some neighbors. After administering to her severe wound, the men went off in search of the Shawnee brave. The brave was tracked down and killed by the men. Elizabeth eventually healed and wore a black bonnet to hide the scar for the rest of her life.

The DeWitt log cabin still stands. It is the oldest remaining structure in the township. It may also harbor Elizabeth's ghost. People have reported a

The DeWitt Log Homestead sits outside of Oxford and may still harbor the spirit of the scalped Elizabeth DeWitt. *Author's collection.*

presence felt in the cabin. Some say it's angry or sad. A story in the 1930 *Sandusky Register* said that "the tale of Mrs. Elizabeth Dewitt runs rampant each Halloween." The article also alludes to her still wandering the grounds of their farmstead, at that time the Oxford Retreat Farm.

Fairfield's Haunted Mansion

The Elisha Morgan Mansion is a two-story Federal-style brick home originally built in 1817 by Elisha Morgan. David Hueston obtained the land in 1849. He constructed the historic Greek Revival addition to the house in 1858. These two different styles were the prevalent styles used in nineteenth-century Ohio. The mansion is an excellent representation utilizing the two predominant styles of the rural past in Fairfield Township and Butler County. The Ross family purchased it in 1871. By 1875, they had a very successful vineyard and fruit farm, as shown in the *1875 Atlas of Butler County*. Ross Road, where the house sits, is named after them. Alonzo Ross and his wife sold the property in 1880 but bought back sixty acres, including the

Sketch from the *1875 Butler County Atlas* showing the home and farm buildings when the property was owned by the Ross family. *MidPointe Library Local History and Genealogy Collection.*

house, in 1883. It stayed in the family until 1916, six years after Alonzo died. It was enshrined on the National Register of Historic Places in 1990.

Heidi Schiller was the manager of the Fairfield Community Arts Center from late 2005 until late 2019. One of the things the center did was handle rentals for the Elisha Morgan Mansion. The mansion is frequently rented out for small weddings, rehearsal dinners and other events. Heidi was there frequently and conducted tours for prospective renters. One day, as she was taking an engaged couple through the house, as they walked from one room into another on the upper floor, the soon-to-be groom suddenly stopped, and Heidi saw all the color drain from his face. She asked if he was OK, and he replied, "There is something wrong with this room." He said that he felt a wave of intense cold, then he became so unnerved that he had to leave. Needless to say, they didn't use the building for their wedding. As Heidi went to straighten everything up before she left, she started to complain to the ghosts that their antics cost her a rental. As she went back to the upstairs room, checking the locks, she felt like a sheet of cold air hit her right in the face. She also added that there were no open windows or any vents in that area.

One year after Christmas, folks were taking down the ornaments from the tree and placing them on a table. The next day, the ornaments on the table had been moved; some were even found on the floor upstairs. It seems the spirits were wanting to celebrate the full twelve days of Christmas!

A maintenance worker in the parks department shared a story about something strange happening with the alarm system. He had received a call from the alarm company at three o'clock in the morning saying that one of the interior motion sensor alarms had been set off. They went on to say that none of the exterior door alarms had been activated. An interior door was opening and closing, causing the motion sensor to go off.

One time, a group of ghost hunters was allowed to see if they could find anything to substantiate the stories. The investigators asked Heidi if they could investigate the basement, which is not accessible to the public. The group set up cameras and placed a bottle on the floor. They would ask questions, and the bottle would rotate. They asked if Elizabeth Morgan, Elisha's second wife, was in the room, and the bottle began to move. They asked if Sarah, Elisha's first wife, was there, and the bottle flew out of camera range. It looked like it had been kicked. After one investigation, when everything was turned off and locked up, someone outside noticed the basement light had turned back on.

Another time, during a public ghost hunt, a couple asked Heidi what used to be behind the house and pointed to the area near where a playground

The Morgan Mansion as it looks today. *Author's collection.*

is currently located. The woman saw a man standing out there in the field in clothes reminiscent of late 1800s farming attire. Heidi replied that that was where the old barn stood. She wondered out loud if that was Joseph Ross, who, as legend had it, died in or near the barn, possibly purposely or accidentally shot. It's difficult to find Joseph's history and information about whether he was killed on the site. He was mentioned, with Alonzo, as being in charge of the John Ross estate after their father's passing in 1870. There were a few men with that name in the area at the time, but I found no stories that mention one being shot. Seven Joseph Rosses were buried in Spring Grove Cemetery that fit the timeframe; this is where almost all of the family are buried.

The site today is enjoyed by many, thanks to the efforts of the City of Fairfield in having the foresight to purchase the land in 1980, save and restore the home and create a park. The mansion also plays host to the Fairfield Historical Society, which holds monthly meetings there with some great guest speakers. There are plenty of areas to walk around and have a picnic, and maybe you'll see an old farmer out in the field.

CRAWFORD'S DAUGHTER

In 1835, David and Jeanette Crawford built their house, calling it the Forest Cottage. They used native fieldstone taken from the nearby creek, now known as Crawford's Run. Hancock Avenue was there when the house was built, named the Road to Chester at the time.

Today's East Hamilton neighborhoods were farm fields to the west of the house. After David Morgan passed away in 1881, the house went to his son, David, who then left it to his son, William, in 1909. William lived there until his passing in 1947. Shortly after, two grandchildren, Robert Falconer and Mary Cavanaugh, donated the land and home to the City of Hamilton; on the passing of Mary Cavanaugh, the city would assume ownership of the home. She passed away in 1958. After the city took control of the home, some of the park attendants and their families lived in the house for a couple years, then it was left vacant. By 1960, the house was already 125 years old. It sat unused, near dark woods on a dark road, near neighborhoods full of kids who loved to explore. By 1966, the once-beautiful home had been ransacked by vandalism. Through preservation actions by many groups, the house was renovated and rededicated in 1967.

The Crawford Home and Farm as it looked in a sketch from the *1875 Butler County Atlas*. The view would be from current Hancock Avenue looking southeast. *MidPointe Library Local History and Genealogy Collection.*

The ghost stories started after the house became vacant in the early 1960s. People would hear a young girl playing and singing old nursery rhymes in the woods, although no one ever saw the girl. That is, they never saw her in the woods. People claimed to see a young girl looking down from the upper window, and that girl was Mary Crawford.

David and Jane Crawford had four children; Mary was the only daughter. She was born on October 20, 1846, and passed away on October 3, 1852. She was born in that house and probably died in that house. It was all she knew, and perhaps she was looking out at the other children enjoying her old home. A legend began to spread that David Crawford was so distraught over losing his beautiful little girl that he couldn't bury her. One story said that he hid her body in the attic, which is why she is seen looking out that window. Another said she was buried near the house. However, she is buried with her family in Greenwood Cemetery.

There have been other stories where people feel like they are being followed while walking in the woods, hearing footsteps behind them. There could be many reasons, but a curious article in the March 17, 1859 *Weekly*

The Crawford Home as it stands in 2023, awaiting restoration work. *Author's collection.*

Hamilton Telegraph points to one possibility. Thirty-five-year-old John Farrell's body was found on the Crawford Farm. He had purposely drunk himself to death and died of exposure. He was found with half a bottle of whiskey and a note asking for his wages and clothes to be donated and his wife to be notified that he died. Perhaps this poor lost soul still wanders the area, looking for peace.

The house is again in a state of disrepair, but many local groups are working to restore it to its glory. The windows have been covered, so no one can see if Mary is looking out the window anymore.

MORE SPIRITS OF HUESTON WOODS

In 1950, the state acquired more land for Hueston Woods State Park, including the Doty farm. The state rehabbed the home for use as an administrative building during construction of Acton Lake. The house, known as the Doty Homestead, was built beginning in 1832 by James Morris. Up to that point, the land had changed hands a couple times, but no one had built anything on it. Morris began the slow process of digging clay on-site and baking bricks. According to the local folklore, he dug a cave adjacent to the building to live in while the house was being built; "that cave" eventually became the root cellar and still exists on-site. In 1842, Morris fell into hard times, and the home went to creditors. Samuel Doty, Morris's brother-in-law, purchased the property in 1844. As other farms and cabins were built in the general vicinity of the Doty farm, the area around the homestead became known as the Doty Community.

Besides the farm, relics from these days include the Doty Road, which still ends at the home and, just to the south, the Doty Cemetery. The barn was on the site until it burned down in 1980. It was soon replaced with a building matching the Doty period, believed to be from the 1840s. In the summer of 1959, the Doty Homestead opened to the public. Rehabilitated and now full of period antiques, as was the barn, it quickly became a popular attraction. The Doty buildings are owned by the state, but they are managed under the nonprofit Oxford Museum Association, which also operates the DeWitt log cabin, mentioned earlier. The cemetery is owned and maintained by Oxford Township who works with the Oxford Museum Association in a partnership on restoration and other efforts.

The three major areas of the Doty Settlement have reported paranormal events. In the Doty Homestead, people have heard voices and seen shadows.

The Doty Homestead, originally built by Joseph Morris (circa 1836) and purchased by Samuel Doty in 1844. It was a working farm until the 1950s, when it was incorporated into Hueston Woods State Park. *Author's collection.*

Also, multiple people have felt the sensation of being touched or their hair being played with. An apparition has been seen standing near a display case on the first floor of the barn. People have felt uneasy on the upper floor among the farm equipment. With the barn being from another location and full of historic artifacts, it's unknown if the apparition or other experiences are tied to the land or to an artifact. The home is also filled with many items from various sources.

The cemetery, called the Doty Settlement Cemetery or the Oxford Township Cemetery, had its first burial in 1843: that of Sarah "Mary" Smith, the wife of Job Smith. Job Smith then deeded that one acre of land in 1844 for a cemetery and church. The last burial was recorded in 1934. Although many grave markers are missing, buried, destroyed or eroded away, it is believed there have been about one hundred burials. The 1905 *Centennial History of Butler County, Ohio* states that a twenty-four-by-thirty-six frame church was started but never finished. The cemetery also holds the grave of Samuel Doty, who passed away in 1859. His first wife, the sister of the man who built the house, Sarah (Morris) Doty, is also buried there. People have stated they have heard whispers, and a paranormal group had an electronic triggering device, which is designed to light up when touched, set off by something as it was on the ground, according to a *Journal News* article.

CHAPTER 3
SPIRITED SETTLEMENTS

HAUNTINGS IN OHIO'S OLDEST TAVERN

Butler County is proud to lay claim to the oldest tavern in the state. It has a storied history, with high-spirited owners and colorful cast of characters that have been through the doors for over two hundred years. When Abraham Darr opened it in 1817, he probably didn't dream it would be still operating in the twenty-first century. Today, the tavern is known as the Hitching Post. It's a fitting name for a tavern that was originally on a drover's path, as it gave the drovers a place to hitch their horses as they stopped at the tavern. Drovers were the men who "drove" the livestock—typically pigs, in Butler County—to the larger cities, and Darrtown was on the route from western Ohio and eastern Indiana to Cincinnati. The inns and taverns offered not only the men a bit of respite but also the hogs, as many would offer yards or pens for the hogs and rooms and refreshments for the men.

In the 1830s, it became faster for the farmers to send their hogs to Cincinnati by way of canals. With increased stagecoach traffic, the roads were widened, straightened and leveled to allow for better and faster travel. The Hamilton to Richmond turnpike, on which Darrtown was a stop, began construction in 1838. This became known as the Darrtown Pike. Abraham sold the Hitching Post in 1851. It then passed through five owners over the next forty-eight years until the Shuck family bought it in 1899; they owned it until 1925. During their tenure, they saw the change from stagecoach to

Dodge touring car on Darrtown Pike from 1915, probably heading to the Hitching Post! *Lane Public Library, George C. Cummins "Remember When" Photograph Collection.*

automobile. Hitching Post customers' method of travel changed, but the tavern was still there to offer a stopover for food and drink. It changed hands a couple more times until it was taken over by Earl "Red" Huber.

According to the local history website www.darrtown.com, run by local historian Fred Lindley, it was thought Red took over in 1949, but a liquor license in his name was found dated 1944. Red was the most popular owner of the tavern. He lived above the bar and reportedly had peepholes in his floor to keep an eye on things. He passed away in 1982, and he is still talked about favorably by those who knew him and those who wished they knew him. He was very well known for his Christmas parties and his friendship with local legend and member of the National Baseball Hall of Fame Walter "Smokey" Alston.

Noted gangster John Dillinger is said to have visited the bar frequently and was friendly with the owners at the time, the Wiley family, as Dillinger allegedly was known to hideout at a nearby farm. In 1971, Red and two of his employees, Pat Davis and Ethel Leugers, faced a very scary situation.

Four men came into the bar around ten thirty on a Tuesday night; they sat at a rear table and drank until one thirty. As they went to leave, they tied Red up, taped his eyes and mouth shut, and robbed the place. With the help of Pat Davis, Red was freed of his bonds, and one of the men grabbed Ethel Leugers and fled with her, $193 in cash and two pistols. They released Ethel when they reached their car and sped off. Thankfully, no one was seriously injured.

Sadly, in 1982, Red passed away, at eighty-six years of age, upstairs in his room. The building has been around for over two hundred years, with countless individuals entering the establishment, and there are many types of energy flowing through its wooden frame. Strange phenomena have been witnessed by the people who work and visit there. Many think at least one may be Red.

Tasha and Pat Cain purchased the Hitching Post in 2014. Tasha only had one experience herself: as she turned off the lights one night, one turned back on. She thought it may have been a short in the wiring, but she checked the switch, and it had flipped to the "on" position. Their daughter, Kirsten, has had a few strange occurrences of her own. On two occasions, as she was standing by the pool table, she saw a man in the bathroom washing his hands. The first time was before the Hitching Post opened. She said it was

The Hitching Post in Darrtown has stood in the same location since 1817. *Author's collection.*

a tall, skinny, dark human shape with no discernable face. Another night, she was in the upstairs office, and the door to the room slammed shut. A different time, she was in the room across from the office and fell asleep. She woke up and, in the darkness, heard distinct footsteps coming from across the hall. Mediums have visited, and one mentioned that Red liked how they were taking care of his place. Some of the current customers have said that previous owners mentioned strange things that happened under their watch. Bartenders have witnessed glasses and bottles fly off shelves; some female workers have been smacked on the rear. One evening a bartender called Tasha and said she wasn't able to finish up her closing duties that night because she had to leave. All the bottles and glassware on the shelves had started shaking, spooking her. It seems a lot of the incidents happen after hours, which makes one wonder if it isn't Red checking up on things; after all, he did tell the medium he liked how the Cains were operating the place.

The Cains sold the Hitching Post in October 2022. The new owners, Britt Colson and Evan Cusmano, took over without missing a beat. Britt actually worked at the Hitching Post before becoming part owner. Both owners continue to hear activity from the men's bathroom. After closing around three o'clock one morning, as Britt was cleaning the women's bathroom, she heard voices coming from the men's room. She waited, expecting someone to walk out, and when no one did, she went in, only to find it empty. Another time after closing, around four o'clock in the morning, as Evan was cashing out at the bar, he heard footsteps walking out of the bathroom; again, no one was there. The new owners are excited to continue the Darrtown tradition of hospitality and service to the community. They have been enjoying getting to know the locals better, and they are happy to welcome everyone, including Red.

The Haunting of Hangman's Hollow

In October 1851, four young men from Darrtown, Taylor Marshall, Ben Scott, Chambers Flenner and Dan Warwick, journeyed by horseback to the inaugural Butler County Fair in Hamilton. The county fair was held near present-day Sixth and High Streets; it would move to the new Butler County Fairground in 1856. That evening on their return trip, they noticed a small group of people along the edge of the road. Someone had found a body hanging in the trees. The man was found hanging from a tree with his suspenders wrapped around his neck instead of a rope, an apparent suicide. The condition of the corpse also appeared as if the body had been out in the elements for quite a few days. No one could identify him. A few days later, after inquiries by the sheriff around town, the body was believed to be that of a stockman. He had been in a hotel in Hamilton that week and left saying he had business with farmers in the western part of the county. He had also been openly flashing cash around town at various establishments. It was deduced that he didn't commit suicide but probably was followed to the old hollow and murdered and robbed. The hanging was a ruse to make it look like suicide. There were never any arrests or even suspects in the case. It was said that travelers on the road at the hollow began seeing a shape in the woods, the ghostly shape of a man hanging in a tree. Others heard a ghostly hoarse voice, coming from the woods warning the passersby of the dangers on the road.

Hangman's Hollow is still located just west of the intersections of Old Oxford and Gardner Roads at Hamilton-Richmond Road. The southern side is still heavily wooded, though it's a noticeably different area since the road was raised. There haven't been any tales from there for generations; maybe the ghost decided the paved two-lane road was less prone to bandits.

CHAPTER 4
GILDED AGE GHOSTS

THE HAUNTING LEGACY OF MIDDLETOWN'S FIRST MULTIMILLIONAIRE

The last quarter of the nineteenth century was called the Gilded Age, as it brought increased industry, wage growth and economic growth. Paul John Sorg was a shining example. His rags-to-riches story changed the face of Middletown and still inspires the people of the area. He became one of Middletown's most prominent businessmen. It began when Sorg and John Auer started a tobacco business in Cincinnati. A few years and mergers later, in 1870, they started the P.J. Sorg Tobacco Company in Middletown. They named their top-of-the-line brand Big and Best, and it must have been, because it made them multimillionaires and became one of the largest tobacco firms of the time. From here, Sorg branched out into other profitable ventures. Eventually he even became a member of Congress.

In 1876, Middletown's wedding of the year was undoubtedly Sorg's marriage to Susan Jennie Gruver. In 1888, they moved into their grand home, known as the Sorg Mansion, on South Main Street in Middletown. The million-dollar thirty-five-room mansion, designed by Hannaford & Sons out of Cincinnati, is a Romanesque masterpiece. Now under private ownership, it is occasionally open for public events and tours and well worth the visit. There were stories and rumors of the house being haunted when it was split into apartments and businesses, but nothing ever substantiated these claims.

Sorg was involved in everything from railroads to paper mills to banking. He also turned his eyes toward community involvement and development when he planned and funded the building of the Sorg Opera House. Sorg hired the same architectural firm who designed his house to design the opera house and the commercial buildings attached.

The entry to the Sorg Opera House building is flanked by two commercial buildings. One of these actually houses a ballroom on its upper floor. The rest was used for offices and commercial operations. People have seen shadows walking around in the commercial parts of the building. They have also heard the voices of employees from years past.

Industrialist Paul J. Sorg in 1906. *MidPointe Library Local History and Genealogy Collection.*

When you first enter through the doors of the Sorg Opera House, you'll see a bar area to your right. There have been some strange encounters in this area. Patrons see someone standing behind the bar, but on second glance, no one is there. As you walk through the hallway toward the stage, you'll notice the large portrait of the theater's namesake, Paul J. Sorg. Continuing through the doorway into the main auditorium, walk up to the stage and turn around to look into the front row of the lower balcony. It's said that Mr. Sorg still likes to observe performances from his favorite seat in the opera house. Now turn your attention to the stage. Listen for the phantom footsteps of performers and stagehands that are still working on the shows long since gone. Also cast your gaze to the catwalk above. People still hear former workers above the stage, even when the theater is empty. Now venture to the stairs leading below the stage to the dressing rooms. While walking down the stairs, listen carefully for the voice of a long-lost performer practicing her singing. It may be the woman in a red dress who has been seen and heard below the stage, preparing for her ghostly performance. Some versions have said her dress is blue, or maybe there are two spirits. The final area to visit in the opera house is the upper balcony. When the theater opened, this area was for African Americans only. The entry was by an exterior doorway and stairs. This area was sealed up for quite a while and hidden from view for decades. This was the so-called peanut gallery, a term coined during the days of vaudeville shows; they were the cheap seats. Peanuts were the cheapest snack at the

Sorg Opera House as it looked in 1895. South Main Street was a dirt road at that time. *George C. Crout Collection, MidPointe Library System.*

theater. Aside from the shadow of a man being seen in the upper balcony, some people have said that peanuts have also been found on the floor or on the benches in this area. Maybe some spirits like to snack while watching the current goings-on, even a century later. There was at least one death in the Sorg; surprisingly, it has not been attached to a ghost story. In 1894, a drunken William Poling burst through a door on the outside of the building. Unbeknownst to him, it was the door to the coal room, and he fell fourteen feet into the coal pit. The impact fractured his skull and killed him.

An 1892 view from the stage. From this view, Paul Sorg's seat was in the center on the left-hand side of the aisle in the first row of the balcony—where some say he still can be sometimes seen. *George C. Crout Collection, MidPointe Library System.*

To get away from the heat of the city in the summer, Sorg had a summer home built north of town. It was modeled after their home in Lakewood, New York, along Lake Chitauqua, with its high ceilings, large rooms and outstanding ventilation allowing for excellent air circulation in the days before air-conditioning. According to local historian George Crout, who referred to the home as Grace's Mansion after Sorg's daughter-in-law, one evening, a maid tripped and fell down the rear servants' stairs. She was said to have been a beautiful young girl. It was believed that the strange sounds heard from the basement after her death during the day were made by her, as her spirit threw stones into the old cistern. People would claim to see a woman lit by the glow of a candle in the windows when the home was supposedly empty. In the evenings, she could be seen peering out the windows of the home, especially in the winter months, as, it being a summer home, she was left alone throughout the darkness and cold of the winter. A recent owner has said they heard things from the servant's stairway. A friend felt someone tap them on the shoulder, and knowing the stories, they took a photo and captured a strange white blur. Research has yet to find a source corroborating the story of the Ghost of Grace's Mansion, but there are

THE SORG PAPER COMPANY
MIDDLETOWN, OHIO

The sprawling Sorg Paper Company circa 1950. *George C. Crout Collection, MidPointe Library System.*

many historic happenings that could be the possible causes for the hauntings in another Sorg property.

Sorg sold his tobacco business in 1898 for $4.5 million, and with those funds, he purchased a Middletown paper mill and renamed it the Paul A. Sorg Paper Co. for his son, who would become its president. At that time, he was more vested in his banking, real estate and railroad businesses, so he turned the reins over to his son to run the paper mill. The paper mill building was one of the earliest built in Middletown, dating to 1852 when John Erwin and his brothers created the Middletown Paper Mill. The Sorg Paper Company continued to operate until 2000, when it was shut down. The Wausau Paper Corporation continues to use part of the old mill. Throughout the years, people have claimed the old mill building is haunted. Security guards have claimed to hear footsteps when no one is in the building. They have also seen shadows walking in the corridors. Former and current employees have had occurrences of lights going on and off and doors slamming shut. What could be the cause of these disturbances? It's a dangerous environment and has a long history of injuries and fatalities on the job, some natural and some accidental. In November 1919, John Arpp, a local businessman and contractor, was crushed to death in the elevator when a gate fell, hitting him in the head, then pinning and crushing him between the elevator and the third floor. Horrifically, Wilmus Letney suffocated under a load of paper pulp in 1925. John Bauer of Newport, Kentucky, was electrocuted installing electrical equipment in 1928. Laura Hayes filed suit and won after her husband, a plumber, died when a floor collapsed under him in 1929.

There have also been many serious injuries, from spinal damage from falls to severe electric burns to amputations as limbs get caught in the massive paper-making machinery. Also, with a building in operation for so long, people passing away on the job due to health reasons is something that happens. Robert Zecher, an assistant mill foreman, dropped dead from a heart attack during his shift in 1925. In 1927, Henry Koehler was eating lunch when he collapsed and died after suffering a hemorrhage. Any one of these incidents, plus others, could be the cause of the hauntings.

The Sorg Paper Mill is not the only haunted paper mill in the area. Just south of Middletown, in the village of Excello, the Harding-Jones Paper Company was located between the canal and the railroad to allow for ease of shipping its popular paper products. Excello was actually the brand name of its paper, which is where the name of the mill and the town that sprang up nearby originated. The paper mill began operation in 1865 under A.E.

The main building at the Harding-Jones Paper Mill, 1996. *Roger L. Miller Collection, MidPointe Library System.*

Harding, who came from a family of English paper makers. In 1853, he came to Middletown to work at the Middletown Paper Mill. His son-in-law, Thomas Jones, took over the business after Harding's death. He renamed it the Harding-Jones Paper Company. The area is actually designated a National Historic District, although you really wouldn't know it. The district includes the lock, the mill building and two of Harding's homes. It was purchased by the Simpson Paper Company in the early 1980s, and it closed in 1990. The mill sat derelict until it was demolished in 2018. However, those who have entered the abandoned building claim to have witnessed some paranormal events: hearing voices, seeing shadows. One person claimed to see a woman in a window. All that remains now is some rubble and a smokestack, but the mill site may soon be part of a park trail system.

Visit www.sorgoperahouse.org for upcoming shows. Search "Dayton Haunted Explorers" on Facebook for haunted events at the Sorg Opera House.

HAUNTINGS IN THE BANK

There is a lot of Middletown history on the southwest corner of South Main and Central Avenue. Stephen Vail, one of the founders of Middletown, built his log cabin here. Vail and his ten children from three marriages came to Ohio from New Jersey; they were some of the earliest people to settle in the area, around 1800. Vail and his family owned much of the land around what would become downtown Middletown. He was one of the men who set about laying out the city, and this was to be one of the main intersections. When the canal arrived in 1825, the city really grew as the canal connected the area to Lake Erie in the north and the Ohio River to the south. Area farmers would bring their merchandise to town to sell or ship. There was a lot of money changing hands and nowhere to keep it safe. According to the *Centennial History of Butler County*, most farmers would "bank" with their millers or other purchasers.

As industries grew up around the river and canal, people needed the necessities. William B. Oglesby and George C. Barnitz had a general store on the spot. The Oglesby and Barnitz General Store became a place where farmers would gather, meet and also purchase items they needed. The Oglesby and Barnitz store became a mainstay on the journey to the town, and the store owners became friends with many farmers and tradesmen in the area. They also supplied banking services. In 1847, with the growth of their banking side and seeing the need for legitimate banking operations, Oglesby and Barnitz decided to open an actual bank of deposit and exchange inside the store. This was one of the first banks in the area.

Banking was a great business move by the men. The bank operated out of the first-floor portion of the building that sat on the corner until 1888. They continued their general goods sales utilizing the second story and the rest of the first. William B. Oglesby passed away in 1885, passing his duties to his son. The banking industry continued to grow, and in 1889, the operation was incorporated as the Oglesby & Barnitz Company, Bankers. That same year, a new three-story brick building was constructed on the same corner. When George C. Barnitz passed away in 1894, his son took over his part of the operation. The company reorganized again in 1925 and was rechristened the Oglesby-Barnitz Bank and Trust Company. Shortly thereafter, in 1929, the building was replaced with the grand structure that still stands today. Eventually, through mergers and buyouts, it became Bank One and then Chase Bank and, in 2000, had its doors closed after more than 150 years.

The building reopened after fifteen years in 2015 and now serves as a wonderful event center in the heart of Middletown named the Windamere. Mica Glaser-Jones and Theron Jones purchased the building before they were married and held their first event four months later in October 2015. The name comes from a farm in New Zealand that the grandmother of a business partner of the owners grew up on. They found the name elegant but not pretentious, which was perfect for the event space. In preparation for the opening, they undertook a renovation that included repairing plasterwork and adding restrooms and a kitchen. They tried to reuse anything that had to be removed or was found in storage, especially anything that was original to the building. The wall sconces are original to the 1929 building; the chandelier, however, has a different place of origin. It was originally located in one of Cincinnati's most haunted buildings, Music Hall. The elegant chandelier hangs from the forty-foot ceiling, bookended by balconies on either end, and overlooks the former bank lobby and current event hall. Today the building bustles with great energy as people celebrate weddings, parties and other events in the former banking institution. But even though the building sat silent and empty for a decade and a half, maybe it wasn't quite that empty.

When Mica and Theron were doing renovations, they had a feeling they weren't always the only ones there. A friend who was a paranormal investigator asked if he could check the place out. He brought a medium with him. One of the first impressions the medium received was from a woman named Alice O. She could not quite get the last name; she said it was strange-sounding and began with an *O*. It seems like she had contacted or been contacted by Alice Oglesby, socialite and wife of Charles Barnitz Oglesby, a former president of the bank and son of the founder. The medium also had a feeling in a corner of a room about a man who had a heart attack. Coincidentally, at a later time, a different medium had the same feeling about a man having a heart attack. However, one of the mediums said the man died and the other said the man lived. Strangely, history shows that they were both right. On March 10, 1922, Joseph R. Shafor died of "heart trouble" at ten o'clock in the morning. The *Akron Beacon Journal* callously ran with the garish headline "Banker Drops Dead." On August 27, 1938, W.O. Barnitz, son of the founder and the president of the bank at that time, died at his home after having a heart attack at the bank the previous Saturday. Russell Weatherwax was president of the bank when he had a heart attack while on a business trip in 1954. He recovered and lived until 1971.

One of the mediums also saw a tall, dark man in the corner of the main hall. She said he looked at her, smiled and tipped his hat. The medium was also receiving an extremely odd visual cue. She asked Mica, "Do you remember the sitcom in the '80s with the alien puppet?" Mica replied, "Do you mean Alf?" The medium said she kept seeing that image, so they thought maybe the man was named Alf. Sometime later, the Middletown Historical Society gave Mica a copy of a photo of the original building on the site. She saw a tall man in a hat and showed it to the medium, and she gasped, saying that looked like the man she saw. The 1887 photo shows five men in front of the bank building. Standing on the far right is a tall, dark man in a hat, labelled as Alf Johns—Alpha U. Johns to be exact. He was a prominent farmer in the Miltonville area and later owned a cigar factory in Trenton.

The basement is an enormous maze of rooms, and there are some that Mica said she does not feel comfortable being in; she explains it as feeling like she's "going through muck." Others also have had strange feelings in the basement areas. While Mica was taking two women through the building, they passed through one of these areas in the basement hallway that made Mica feel uneasy. The women, who were with a religious organization looking to book the Windamere for a church event, apparently felt the same thing. They asked her if they could pray, and she told them they could. Mica left the room, and as the women were praying, she felt ice

The original building of Oglesby & Barnitz, Bankers from 1887. The man on the far right in the hat is Alpha Johns, whom a visitor believed they saw over one hundred years later. *George C. Crout Collection, MidPointe Library System.*

cold, and goosebumps appeared on her arms. As soon as she felt this, the women walked out and said they both felt ice cold and were also covered in goosebumps. It is thought that some of the negative energy may be residual from the time the building was abandoned.

In another part of the basement, a medium kept sensing well-dressed men in dress shoes—probably not that strange, given the presence of bankers and executives in the building, except she also sensed mafia ties. There actually may be a reason for it. On November 28, 1944, John Erb, a teller at the bank, along with Arthur Miltonberger, the bank custodian, drove to the nearby post office. They pulled into a parking space, turned off the car, and suddenly their doors were pulled open and guns were pointed in their faces. Four armed men had appeared out of nowhere; two stood on either side of the car and the other two covered the men inside. According to the *Dayton Herald*, one of the men said, in true gangster fashion, "Don't move. Turn it over or we'll let you have it." He was demanding a satchel that contained $30,000 disguised by being wrapped in newspaper. The money was to have been shipped to the Federal Reserve in Cincinnati. The man grabbed the bag of money and ran across the street with his accomplice; the other two men had already crossed and started the engine of their black sedan. They sped away, heading north. The two bank employees both saw the number of the license plate, which was later found to have been stolen. The strangest part was how the robbery went perfectly. Normally, Erb would have walked the money alone, but today, he and Miltonberger drove; Miltonberger went along to assist Erb in picking up a load of silver for the bank. The gangsters seemed to have known when and how the money would arrive at the post office.

Very few people in the bank knew when the transfer was happening, as transfers didn't happen at specific times because of the threat of robberies. According to the *Chillicothe Gazette*, Detective Howard Smith said that the robbery was accomplished with a precision indicating a professional job. A break in the case came when Indianapolis police arrested Anthony Demarco on a grand larceny charge in January 1945. He would not turn over the names of his accomplices to the police or the FBI. On March 8, 1945, two more men, Joseph Mendino and Leonard Gianola, both of Chicago, were arrested. A month later, they were released, as the assistant U.S. attorney said there was insufficient evidence against them. Whatever became of Demarco is unknown. Is it possible the heist was coordinated in the basement of the bank?

The basement also houses a room that the Middletown Historical Society uses for storage. At one point, there was a charter school in a portion of the basement. The friend who was a paranormal investigator decided to investigate the "guys' room" in the basement, a room used as a hangout for Theron and his friends. People have claimed to feel "something" in that room, so he decided to lie down on a couch and record audio to see if he could capture any evidence. Surprisingly, he captured the voice of a little girl saying, "Daddy?" It's not known who the girl was or why she was there. Was she a former charter school student?

There has been a great variety of types of activity in the building on all floors. The upstairs main ballroom has one unique feature: the former bank vault is now a bar. What a way to keep the liquor secure! Although it may not be too secure, because a ghostly woman in white has been seen entering the vault. Maybe it's the socialite Alice Oglesby looking to lighten the mood? One of the balconies is used as the VIP area and also hosts a grand piano. Mica says her mother prefers to avoid the balconies because she has had strange feelings up there. One afternoon while setting up for an event, someone was heard tinkling on the piano keys; of course, no one was up on the balcony. Another afternoon, Mica and her dog were in her office when she heard a woman speaking—not just a word or two but what sounded like unintelligible sentences. At the same instant she heard the

Right: This new three-story structure was built in 1890 on the site of the previous building. *George C. Crout Collection, MidPointe Library System.*

Below: The Oglesby-Barnitz Bank and Trust Company building, circa 1938. *George C. Crout Collection, MidPointe Library System.*

ethereal speaking, her dog jumped up and ran out of the room barking. Nothing was found on the security tapes. Yet another mystery from inside this enigmatic gem in the center of Middletown.

If you would like to have your event in a beautiful, yet haunted building, view the information on its website, www.thewindamere.com, which also has links to its Facebook page and information on other events, including Mica's ghost tour. The South Main Ghost Tour is a walking tour where you hear about the strange happenings in some of Middletown's historic residential treasures.

The Haunted Elevator

George Rentschler was an industry leader in an industrial city. He came to Hamilton with little and eventually changed the city in big ways, especially when he decided to build Hamilton's first skyscraper. The eight-floor building was a mammoth in downtown Hamilton in 1906 that housed a bank and offices. Workers in the building have heard tales from its past. Deanna Schneider worked in a law office there, and she said they would hear strange things when in the office alone. She was told by the building superintendent that an elevator attendant had a heart attack between floors five and six. Even though the elevators in the Rentschler Building don't have attendants anymore, people have said they have seen the man. Sometimes the elevators move on their own. They have been known to spontaneously travel to a random floor, whether anyone was on them or not. There are no records of an elevator operator dying on the elevator. However, there are records of an extremely popular elevator attendant who passed away unexpectedly at his home. Joseph Tuley seemed to be a favorite of everyone. As one of the elevator attendants in the Rentschler Building for many years, he was a well-known fixture in Hamilton. When he passed away in July 1925, his obituary was on the society page. A decade later, his passing was mentioned in the July 1935 10 Years Ago column. Maybe Mr. Tuley is still working the elevators to this day.

The building actually has two elevators, and it may have two ghosts. In August 1907, a ten-year-old boy, Merville Hall, became dizzy as the south elevator car he was in passed the third floor. He fell against the glass door, which shattered, and he fell into the shaft. He landed headfirst and died of a broken neck. Could this tragic accident have been the impetus for the

A photo from 1906 of the Rentschler building in downtown Hamilton, the first "skyscraper" in town. *Lane Public Library, George C. Cummins "Remember When" Photograph Collection.*

decades of accidents in the south elevator that came after? In February 1914, the cables snapped, sending the elevator car plummeting from the fourth floor to the basement. Amazingly, it only left several people with cuts, bruises, sprains and one broken leg. In January 1927, a cable broke again; the safety brakes worked, and the cars were stranded between floors. New elevators were installed in the fall of 1930, but in February 1941, the south elevator came crashing again, falling four floors and injuring seven of the eleven passengers on board. Everything seemed to be in working order, and there was no explaining why the safety features did not stop the car. The Warner Company, manufacturers of the safety equipment, said this was the first time in history that their safety appliances did not work when they were needed. Did Merville Hall's tragic accident jinx the south elevator?

Hauntings at the Monroe Historical Society

Monroe was laid out in 1817 and named after the newly elected president James Monroe. Due to its location between Cincinnati and Dayton, it became an important trading center and stop for travelers. Monroe saw a large increase in population from 1950 to 1960, thanks to the construction of I-75. In 1950, Monroe's population was 360 people; by 1960, it was 2,193; and it hasn't stopped since, with its 2020 population reaching 15,412.

When it was a smaller, more farm-oriented town, before the advent of large supermarkets, the person to buy all your groceries, dry goods, hardware and other notions from was Marion Warner. Warner was born in Monroe on Halloween in 1861. That seems a fitting date, since he still makes appearances at the locations where he worked and lived. Throughout the years, the Census has Warner as an artist, druggist and merchant. His keen artistic eye is seen around the Monroe Historical Society in some of his paintings and especially in his photography collection, consisting of many historic photos of Monroe from the late 1800s to the first couple decades of the 1900s. Amazingly, after being lost for decades, the glass negatives were found. After Jim Price's mother bought the house when Nelle Warner passed away in 1969, he found them while cleaning the carriage house in the back. They have been scanned and are available through the Midpoint Library website.

Around town, Marion Warner was known as the man who could provide the town with everything it needed. His home and business were located on the corner of Elm Street and Main Street, also known as Cincinnati-Dayton Road. Where his house used to stand is now the home of the Monroe Historical Society's wonderful museum building. The building, with its long porch dormers, was built in 2000 and based on the Chickahominy House in Williamsburg, Virginia. The house was also built over the foundation of the Warners' home. The Warners had two daughters, Nelle and Bessie, and a son, Carl. Sadly, Bessie passed away in 1892 at only three years of age. There is a framed photo of Bessie in the museum building. As I was being led on a tour with the museum curator, Scott Fowler, he pointed out the photo and said in all his time in the building, he's never seen the picture out of place, yet the previous day it was, and he moved it back. That morning, when he arrived to meet with me, it had been moved yet again.

The Monroe Historical Society has had ghost-hunting groups at the building, and Mr. Fowler has actually been present for some unexplainable events. Sometimes things do seem to have moved from another room, and

A photo by Marion Warner of his home, probably taken around 1910. This is where the Monroe Historical Society Museum currently stands. *Monroe Historical Society, Marion G. Warner Glass Plate Negative Collection.*

sometimes they just move. There is a large heavy cabinet in the dining room, with large heavy candleholders, and during an investigation, they started rattling. No one felt or noticed any vibration that could have caused it, no one was near the cabinet who could have bumped into it and it's never happened since.

Mr. Fowler said the most unbelievable activity that happened took place in the basement. As the group was sitting in a circle, they heard a voice. It sounded like the voice of an old man grumbling; they couldn't quite make out the words, though. The basement is a walkout basement with a window and doors. During this time, some artificial trees were stored in the basement, near the window. People, including Mr. Fowler, saw something invisible walk by the trees and the window; the trees and the curtains both moved as if someone had strolled past them. The window and door were both shut, and there was no one else in that area. That same night, a few people noticed a chill in an area by the fire truck that is on display in the basement. Mr. Fowler did say there was a vent in the ceiling near there but couldn't say if that caused it, as he didn't personally feel it. He did say he

The basement display area of the Monroe Historical Society. At the time when there were artificial trees next to the window, people witnessed the branches and curtains move as if a person had walked past. *Author's collection.*

really wasn't sure if he believed in the ghostly happenings, but after seeing the trees and curtains move like they did, and after hearing the grumbling old man, he thinks more about the possibility that Marion Warner may still be in his old basement, if not elsewhere in the house.

The *Hamilton Evening Journal*, on July 1, 1910, reported on Warner's new building plans: "He has a much larger place, and will handle a larger stock of dry goods, notions, paints and oils and be able to supply the wants of the people." The building has had several makeovers throughout the years: a general store, a soda fountain, a dress shop, a municipal services building, a popular local hangout called the Hornet's Nest and now a museum. The store Warner built for his expanding business sits right on the corner and is appropriately known as the 1910 building. After Mr. Warner died in 1922, his daughter Nelle ran the store for over twenty years. The store does have activity; the most notable occurrence is hearing unintelligible voices, but they're never very clear.

The ghosts of the Monroe Historical Society aren't there because of any tragedy or horrible events. The Warners were everyday working people. Marion Warner was a well-respected man in the community, and it seems

The building that served as Marion Warner's store. Now called the 1910 Building, it holds museum displays and may also hold a ghost. *Author's collection.*

like he may just like keeping an eye on things and making the occasional visit. You can visit the historical society's website, www.monroeohhistoricalsociety. org, or its Facebook page for hours and other information.

THE POOR HOUSE ON THE HILL

The Butler County Infirmary, or as it was locally called, the Poor House, sat off Princeton Road overlooking Hamilton for nearly a century. In 1831, county leaders decided they needed a facility to care for the indigent in the area. The first buildings were built in 1832, followed by a brick "madhouse" built in 1835. In 1884, the county commissioners hired architects to design a large new structure. The Butler County Infirmary was completed and dedicated in 1885. The main building, sheds and barns served as shelter for over 2,500 Hamilton residents during the 1913 flood. In 1974, the facility was losing money from state and federal budget cuts. The third and fourth floors had been closed by the fire marshal and condemned as hazards. Commissioners approved a levy for a new Butler County Home in 1974. The levy passed that fall, and a new building was scheduled to open in 1976. The old building closed in the fall of 1976.

After the closure and relocation of the residents to the new nearby facility, the old building achieved new life in the fall of 1978 as the Hamilton-Fairfield Jaycees Haunted House on the Hill. The haunted attraction became one of the most popular in the Tri-State Area. They even had horror icon Vincent Price record lines for their production. When I was very young, my mom took me to the children's "matinee" haunt, which was geared toward kids, where the monsters would shake your hand and give you high fives instead of jumping out to scare you. I also remember practicing soccer behind Garfield school until dusk in the fall, and as the sunlight faded, you would hear Vincent Price's unique voice echoing over the sports fields: "Welcome to the Hamilton-Fairfield Jaycees Haunted House on the Hiiiiill."

Preservationists worked to protect the structure from further damage and deterioration. Demolition did begin in December 1982. Three hours

An undated photo, probably taken in the 1970s, of the Butler County Infirmary. *Butler County Historical Society.*

later, a work stoppage was ordered by the court. The stay of execution would not last long, as a "mysterious" tragedy occurred on the morning of February 17, 1983. The folks below noticed a glow on the hill in the early morning hours. A fire had erupted in the building. Once firefighters contained and extinguished the blaze, the main central tower and the south wing were so heavily damaged that they were ordered to be razed by fire chief William Heib. The preservationists conceded defeat, as only a portion of the building remained, and that, too, was demolished. The arsonist was never brought to justice.

One story about a demented inmate now seems eerily foreboding. The January 18, 1890 *Cincinnati Enquirer* reported that an "incurable inmate" by the name of Michael Brady was said to have become violently insane and frequently threatened the lives of other inmates and staff, so much so that he was kept locked up at all times. He also threatened that if he ever escaped, he would burn all the buildings of the infirmary to the ground.

The old building had the typical creepy creaks and groans any old structure has, and it also had a ghost. A ghost light was seen in the basement of the building, and the *Journal News* did a story on it years ago. I saved the article, but it has since disappeared, and I have not been able to find it through digital or microfilm searches. The article claimed a light was seen in the basement that seemed to move with purpose. People tried to debunk this in various ways. The *Journal News* article debunked the notion that it was headlights from outside coming through the windows. According to the story that revolved around the light, it was a man who escaped from the confines of the home and died of exposure. There were two accounts. In the first, he was found deceased on the grounds, and in another, he managed to get back through the basement and died there. There are many stories of people—inmates, as they were called in the newspapers—escaping the facility over the years. There are two stories that could account for the legend attached to the ghost light.

According to a *Cincinnati Enquirer* article from August 24, 1894, a farmer south of Middletown came across a body in the woods near his farm. It was the body of a man who had been seen begging in the area recently. The corpse was guarded by a little pug that kept watch over its owner. Authorities had to capture and tie up the dog to be able to access and identify the body. There was nothing to establish the identity of the man; however, the undergarments offered a clue, as they were the type issued at the Butler County Infirmary. The authorities followed up with the infirmary, and they were able to identify the man as seventy-year-old William Loughlin, who

The remains of the stone frieze above the door to the Butler County Infirmary that lie in a garden at the Butler County Historical Society. *Author's collection.*

had wandered away from the home several weeks prior. He had no known relatives and had died of a stroke.

A December 22, 1900, *Dayton Herald* article told a story that seems to coordinate even more closely with the alleged ghost light legend. A man by the name of Michael Smith, referred to as an "aged inmate," was found near death at the edge of an icy pond. It was believed he had been lying there all night after escaping the infirmary. When he was found, he was taken to the hospital, and he died en route.

One of the few remaining vestiges of the building are the remnants of the stone frieze that was located over the entry doors, bearing the name "Butler County Infirmary." The frieze now lies in a garden behind the Butler County Historical Society. It sits like a cenotaph as a memorial for the building that helped so many Butler County residents in their time of need.

HAMILTON'S HAUNTED POWER PLANT

In 1893, the city put a $50,000 bond issue on the ballot for the purpose of building a generating plant, whose sole purpose was to illumine the streets and public areas with electric lighting. Up to that point, the lights were gas, and lamplighters had to go around and light each one individually. As the uses for electricity expanded beyond lighting, and many other industries flourished in Hamilton, there were many additions to the building, in 1920 the city purchased electricity from the Ford plant, to meet the needs. It was decided that a new and much larger power plant was going to be needed to serve the community. In 1929, several kilowatt-producing units—two 3,000 and one 7,800—were put into commission in a brand-new building, just north of the original light plant. Later, more additions were added to meet growing needs. The building, also on the state's historic inventory, generates a lot of power, and it also seems to have generated some ghosts.

The hauntings of the municipal electric plant were even mentioned in a press release by the city when celebrating the American Public Power Association's "Public Power Week" in 2016: "For a number of years, staff and contractors have reported unexplained 'visitors' and other strange occurrences at the City of Hamilton Third Street Power Plant."

A Cincinnati-area paranormal team, Creepy Cincinnati Forensics, would also present their findings at two events at the Lane Library. An October 28, 2016, *Journal News* article elaborated on ghost stories; journalist Mike Rutledge spoke with Gary Nibert, a superintendent of the plant. Some people

The municipal power plant building in Hamilton, Ohio. *Author's collection*.

A view inside the municipal power plant building. *Author's collection.*

inside the plant have seen a man, dirty from coal, still working on machinery in the plant. Individuals have also seen the startling and unexplainable sudden movement of objects. A new alarm system would send alerts late at night after detecting movements, which only showed up as dust swirls on the camera, like an invisible force had walked past. The security alerts became so frequent that Nibert had to disable the alarm sounds so he could sleep at night. Nibert also said that one night, when he was working, his coworker repeatedly thought he saw movement like someone had walked past the door, and he would jump up to see no one there. The ghost-hunting group experienced voices, shadows moving and footsteps in the empty building. There were injuries at the facility over the years, some serious, and the ghost-hunting crew was told by the Butler County Historical Society that one man was accidently killed when he was crushed by a pile of coal.

CHAPTER 5

BREWS AND BOOS

A GHOST AMONG THE ARCHES

When the Junction Railroad was approved in 1849, it would connect Hamilton to Indianapolis. The issue facing the construction was the hill in Rossville. John Earhart's solution was a gradual slope from the east side of the river across a large, high bridge and a viaduct through Rossville consisting of seventeen stone arches, cutting through the hill until the train reached a level grade. Work began in 1853. In 1859, the first stretch of the railroad from Hamilton to Oxford was opened.

Alcohol and beer were important in the growth of Rossville. Located in the southern part of Rossville, the Rossville Brewery began in the mid-1800s and eventually became Martin Mason's Eagle Brewery when he purchased it in 1886. In 1941, it became the last brewery to make beer in Butler County until the Miller Brewery opened in 1991. The brewery was torn down in 1977 due to its deteriorating condition. Also nearby, on the north side of the Arches on C Street, was the Sohngen malthouse, which supplied malt to the breweries in the Hamilton and Cincinnati area. That building is the last standing from Hamilton's beer-brewing heyday. Large business endeavors like these needed workers, and a working-class neighborhood had formed between the river and the Rossville hill. At some point around the beginning of the twentieth century, one of the houses at the corner of today's Arch Street and B Street became a tavern. Today, it is known as the Arches Saloon.

Mathes-Sohngen delivery wagon passing the arches at South B and Arch Street in 1912. *Lane Public Library, George C. Cummins "Remember When" Photograph Collection.*

When Matt Pater bought the establishment and some other buildings in 2020, he brought with him a grand idea to create an entertainment area for the whole family along the South B Street corridor. He told the *Journal News* that when he came to look at the bar before he purchased it, he was offered drugs on three occasions. The area has seen a great turnaround since then, and the Arches Saloon is getting to be a popular establishment in the city. It is also known to have liquid spirits and ghostly spirits.

Matt heard stories from former employees who stopped in after he took ownership. Some of his own employees have also had their own experiences. Many employees, old and new, refuse to go to the basement alone. One even said they would rather quit than go to the basement. Employees have reported being touched or grabbed; one was pulled while on the stairs. The basement is actually divided into two separate sections, with two separate accesses. The walls are probably remnants from earlier structures, possibly enlarged. The earlier buildings, as seen on the older maps, which appear to date to the 1840s, were set back from B Street; the current building sits in line with the rest of the structures on B Street. Records supplied to Matt by Brad Spurlock of the Lane Public Library and Historic Hamilton show the current building, as it stands today, being built probably around 1906 to 1908.

The Arch Saloon as it stands today in the shadows of the stone arches. *Author's collection*.

People have claimed to have heard things coming from the second floor, where there have been apartments since the building was built. People seem to have the most experiences in the basement. Not only have workers claimed that they felt the phantoms in the basement, but some have also claimed that they saw an apparition of a lady in white. She has made her appearance multiple times to people in the basement of the building. One spectral woman, who happened to be missing her head, originated across the street from the Arches Saloon. That story goes back to the Baptist church that sat catty-corner from the saloon. It would have been located on today's A Street. The church was located there at least as early as 1840, according to James McBride's 1840 map of Rossville and Hamilton, where it is specifically called out. Jim Blount recounts in his book *Rossville: Hamilton's West Bank* that the church was haunted by a headless woman and that the stories persisted until at least the late 1880s. Blount believes the church may have been torn down around 1910 or more than likely lost in the 1913 flood. Who this woman was, why she haunted the church or how she lost her head is unknown. Could she be the phantom woman who is seen in Rossville and in the Arches Saloon? Maybe when she was seen in the 1800s, her head was not visible due to whatever factors cause apparitions. Maybe she didn't have the energy or desire to be seen fully at those times.

While there are no names presently associated with the strange ghostly happenings, a medium had told Matt that while the female apparition seemed to be a benevolent spirit, there were some more malevolent spirits there. She believed they were the one or ones responsible for the touching and grabbing.

What other incidents from the land's history could contribute to the spirit of the Arches Saloon? There are a few possibilities. One is the story told in an 1874 article in the *Hamilton Examiner*. A large band of Native Americans encamped on the southern end of Rossville in 1808. While the exact area where the camps were is unknown, the saloon does sit in the south end of Rossville, and Arch Street used to be called South Street, as it was the southern edge of town. It was reported the Native Americans would travel across the ford in the Great Miami to Hamilton and get intoxicated and become "very troublesome" at times. There were also stories of the women of the group needing to carry them back to the camp. Not to play into stereotypes, but could some of these Native American spirits be still lingering in the area—and still wanting drinks?

In the 1800s and early 1900s, many people died in their homes. There are many accounts of people who passed away in their residences, including Civil War veteran and onetime Hamilton mayor John Dirk, who passed away at his residence, which was on the current saloon site, in June 1894. Dirk had traveled to Columbus for a meeting and had been feeling ill. When he returned, the undisclosed illness was much worse. He passed away shortly thereafter, surrounded by family at his residence. Maybe this lifelong Rossville native didn't want to leave the area.

Matt shared the only real experience he personally encountered that he couldn't explain. It happened one evening when they held a ghost hunt in the building. While the group was in the basement, they heard footsteps above them. Matt went up to see who it was and saw no one, then a large speaker on a stand fell over with a deafening sound. He has said that he's been in the bar late at night, four o'clock in the morning, doing the books, and he'll hear a "Hello!" coming from somewhere. He always assumes it's coming from someone out on the street. He also mentioned there were some things that made the employees believe the spirit of a child was in the basement. After a basketball and another toy were placed in the basement, they found that the ball had moved from where it was originally placed. According to Matt, people have said they've felt a loss of breath in the basement, and a ghost-hunting group captured what sounded like growling on audio. He wonders if the years when drug usage was prevalent in the area may have also attracted something. Through Matt's improvements and the city and police, things have never been better in the area. South B Street now connects to the Designated Outdoor Refreshment Areas (DORA) at Main Street, and the area looks to have a bright future.

TALES FROM LITTLE CHICAGO

Butler County has always had a lot of booze flowing through it, from the many distilleries in the early 1800s to the breweries that rose in the mid-1800s. When Prohibition went into effect on May 27, 1919, in Ohio (earlier than it did nationally, on January 17, 1920), Butler County had three large-scale operating breweries. Hamilton had the Martin Mason's Eagle Brewing Company in the Rossville neighborhood. The Cincinnati Brewing Company was located at South Front and Sycamore Streets, where the police station is today. The William Sebald brewery was located in Middletown. Along with other supporting industries, Butler County had over one hundred saloons; Hamilton alone had sixty-six.

Lyman Williams Café at South Fifth and Henry Streets in Hamilton was the only saloon to be open in Butler County on May 26, 1919. *Lane Public Library, George C. Cummins "Remember When" Photograph Collection.*

The first year of Prohibition in Butler County was small-time distillers selling their "Miami Valley Dew"; the city hadn't yet earned its moniker of Little Chicago. The area's first major crime occurred in September 1920, involving the hijacking of $22,000 of legal whiskey that was en route from Cincinnati to New York.

Butler County had many unique circumstances that placed it high on the list for the criminal element. Penalties in Ohio were less stringent than in surrounding states. The rural areas of the county easily harbored many smaller distilleries in the secrecy. Corn and hiding places were readily available. Some areas were just too remote to be searched frequently or without the bootlegger catching wind of an impending raid. There also wasn't enough manpower, so the major roads were not able to be patrolled, and there were a lot of paved roads in the county, which made travel by truck more feasible and faster. Hamilton was also on Route 4, which was part of the direct line of illegal imports coming from Canada. It did bring the criminal element to the area—and notable gangsters.

The Gangster's Ghost

By 1933, Americans had been dealing with the Depression for nearly four years and Prohibition for much longer; it ended in December of that year. People began to think of some criminals as modern-day Robin Hoods— they stood up to the government and took what they wanted—and in the Midwest, no one was more popular than John Dillinger. It is fairly certain that he was in Hamilton; it is known for sure that his gang was holed up in a house on Second Street. Dillinger was in prison in Lima, Ohio, after being arrested in Dayton on September 22. The future Dillinger Gang made their way to Hamilton after they escaped the Indiana State Prison in Michigan City, Indiana, on October 1, 1933. Their escape was orchestrated by Dillinger before his arrest. Dillinger was very familiar with the prison because he had just left there in May, after over eight years of incarceration. This is also where he met the men who would become the Dillinger Gang. However, once Dillinger was released, it being the Depression, he had no job, no prospects—and no desire to work. He went back to what he did best: crime. After being free for four months, however, he was back behind bars. Before his incarceration, he did manage to set a plan in motion to get his friends out. Somehow, he arranged for guns to be smuggled into the prison.

While the authorities were looking for the ten escaped men in northern Indiana, they had fled south. The gang, under the leadership of Harry Pierpont, met up with Dillinger's previous partner, Harry Copeland. They then found out that Dillinger had been arrested. Copeland had already arranged for them to hide out in a house on South Second Street in Hamilton, although he also said it wasn't quite ready. While in Hamilton, they hatched a plan to break Dillinger out of the Lima jail, but first they needed funding, so they decided to do what they knew best: rob a bank. One of the men, Charles Makley, suggested a bank in St. Mary's, Ohio. He was familiar with it because he was from there, and it was also on the way to Lima. The heist was successful and netted them $11,000.

On October 12, 1933, the men arrived in Lima and approached the jail. They told Sheriff Jess Sarber that they were Indiana State Prison officials and were there to transfer Dillinger back to Indiana. The sheriff, who was with his wife and a deputy, asked for the mens' credentials. Pierpont's answer was to shoot him twice. Then Pierpont and Makley beat the wounded sheriff, demanding the keys to Dillinger's cell. The dying sheriff would not capitulate, but his wife gave the men the keys. The men locked up Mrs. Sarber and the deputy, rescued Dillinger and left Sheriff Jess Sarber to die from his wounds. State police investigator Matt Leach figured the Michigan City jailbreak, the St. Mary's bank heist and the Dillinger escape were all connected, and he deduced Pierpont was the brains behind it. In an attempt to cause division in the gang, he called them the Dillinger Gang instead of the Pierpont Gang when speaking to the press. This didn't divide the men, because Pierpont didn't care; however, the name stuck. At this point, the search for the men was getting very intense, and they reportedly decided to split up and rendezvous in Chicago. Around midnight on October 15, a tip reached Officer Leach that his prey was back in Hamilton and that they had fled back to Butler County the same afternoon they broke Dillinger out of prison.

On October 16, 1933, around 120 police officers from Ohio and Indiana, armed with machine guns and tear gas, searched three homes and the area around South Second Street where the gangsters had been hiding out. They recovered a stolen vehicle that they believed the men had used. Then the police followed another lead; this one took them to the Great Miami River and across the Venice (Ross) bridge looking for a camp, according to the *Hamilton Journal News*. The same article also disclosed that some of the men had also been in Venice while they were hiding out on Second Street, before they broke Dillinger out of prison. They had rented a camp on the Hamilton County side of the Great Miami River, paying for a week; however, they only stayed a couple days. This would have been because Copeland said the hideout was not ready. While the officers searched the camp area, they found an abandoned car with Illinois plates. A car had been stolen out of a Dr. Hunter's garage on South Front Street on the night of Saturday the fourteenth. An abandoned car with Illinois plates was also found behind his house. The investigators believed the doctor's car was stolen and the fugitives then ditched the car with the Illinois plates. The doctor's car was recovered along East River Road on the morning of the sixteenth. The running boards and fenders were smashed, and the car was out of gas. The plates had been switched, but the doctor's plates were found in the back seat. The police spoke to the farmer who owned the land, and he said he had rented a camp to men who fit the description of the men who had broken out of the Indiana State Prison.

On October 17, the *Journal News* reported that a piece of paper with the words "Thanks, Mr. Dillinger" was found at the camp cottage. The search was called off because the men were believed to now be out of state. Other reports have members of the gang, including Dillinger, robbing police stations for weaponry, including one in Auburn, Indiana, on the fourteenth and another in Peru, Indiana, on the twentieth.

Located a few blocks from the hideout on South Second Street, and just a block away from where the doctor's car was stolen on the night of Saturday the fourteenth, lies the former Loyal Order of the Moose Hall. The building, built in the early 1920s for the fraternal organization, was constructed behind two existing buildings, one being the original home of the Moose Lodge. The new building was originally known as the Moose Palm Garden and functioned as a dance hall with a stage. As early as 1922, the Moose also held public events, such as the Greater Hamilton Exposition, festivals, dances and benefits. It also had a bowling alley by 1929, as the Ohio Historic Inventory file says that from 1929 to 1934, it was known as the Moose Auditorium and Bowling Alleys. If the stories are true, it also has some ghosts.

In the early part of the twenty-first century, with the rise of ghost-hunting television shows, haunted buildings became marketable as haunted attractions. These are buildings that are rumored to be haunted and open their doors for a fee, allowing anyone to conduct a ghost hunt. For a short time, around 2010, the building was billed as the Haunted Lodge. It even had a website bearing the same name.

Many of the stories about this building were centered on the lower level. Downstairs, people reported seeing dark shadows, and items would be left

Original Loyal Order of the Moose (LOOM) building on the right (date unknown). The remaining building can be seen behind these two buildings. *Lane Public Library George C. Cummins "Remember When" Photograph Collection.*

This photo, dated 1936, shows the two older buildings removed, with a dirt lot in front. This was possibly just after the demolition of the two buildings. *Lane Public Library George C. Cummins "Remember When" Photograph Collection.*

Mugshot and signature of Public Enemy Number One: John Dillinger. *Library of Congress.*

in one area only to be found to have been moved to other locations. Lights would go on and off, and voices would be heard from parts of the building that were thought to be empty. There was a serious injury when a janitor, after turning off the lights for the night, fell four feet, landing on his head and suffering a severe concussion. Maybe he's the ghost that flips the lights on and off? One particular story involved a young lady who died in the building and supposedly still lingers around the stage area. Then the big one, the ghost of John Dillinger, was reportedly seen near a lower-level bar. Could he and his crew have visited the Moose Lodge on one of their excursions in Butler County? It is extremely possible. The Dillinger Gang was definitely placed only eight hundred feet away when they stole the doctor's car. One thing is known: the club was raided in June 1926, and authorities confiscated a staggering 1,800 bottles of homebrew, 180 gallons of mash, 5,000 empty bottles and a bottling machine. An operation like that could have had bigger ties, and the Dillinger Gang could have known about them. Whether Dillinger would choose to haunt a building in Hamilton after his death in 1934 or not, who can say?

Hauntings in the Pavilion

The area around Venice had more than its fair share of illegal activity during the days of Prohibition. The woods and dark roads outside of populated Hamilton provided multiple hiding places for moonshiners and murderers. However, the Venice Pavilion—probably the most popular place in the area, with a long and storied history, seems to have avoided any troubles during that time. The Pavilion is definitely haunted, and now, being full of antiques, it seems to have some extra spirits attached. Strangely, while there has been a lot of deadly gangster activity in the area, none of the spirits in the building seem to date to that period. Newspapers talk about gangland activities in the area, but the owners of the Pavilion at that time either kept their noses clean or knew what palms to grease. Maybe they used the chicken grease from their famous dinners? It was an extremely popular hangout at the time and continued a tradition on that site that continues today.

Jeremiah Butterfield bought eight hundred acres and built the first cabin in the area. It was recorded in the *Centennial History of Butler County* that in 1805–6, the area around Butterfield's cabin was "infested with a band of outlaws, marauders and horse thieves." In the lawless backwoods, Butterfield and some of his fellow pioneers took it upon themselves to bring the villains to frontier justice. Several were killed, and the rest fled the area. Mediums who have visited the Pavilion in more recent times have felt an impression that seemed to stretch back to before the days when the site was the Pavilion, before it was a hotel and even before it was the land of the first tavern or stagecoach stop. A few times, inside the building, mediums have spoken of feeling or seeing men who were being beaten or whipped. Could this have been residual spirits from the gang of outlaws that terrorized the early settlers in the area? Or was it the frontier justice that the pioneers dispensed?

Some of the visions, those of Civil War soldiers, seemed to have come from decades later. Emotions were high in July 1863, as John Hunt Morgan's Confederate cavalry were thought to be making their way toward Hamilton. According to local historian Jim Blount, as Morgan's Raiders were approaching from the west, about six hundred men from the Hamilton Home Guards began marching toward Venice to confront the Raiders. These men were hopelessly outnumbered and outgunned, as Morgan's group consisted of well over two thousand men. Of the Hamilton Home Guard contingent dispatched toward Venice, only half of the six hundred were even armed. Although they had the use of axes and hatchets, as the Home Guard created barricades by cutting hundreds of trees down and blocking the roads toward

Hamilton. The fear and tension grew to its apex as a red glow appeared on the horizon on the evening of the fourteenth. It was from the flames of a burning bridge crossing the Great Miami River ignited by Morgan's Raiders in New Baltimore, three and a half miles from Venice. In the end, luck was with Hamilton and Venice that day, as Morgan chose to avoid the cities and veered to the south and east. Perhaps the mediums picked up on the soldiers' energy from those tension-filled days in 1863.

One of the earliest pioneers to arrive in the area was Dr. Benjamin Clark. Clark platted the town in 1817, and due to the sprawling attractiveness of the area, he gave it the name of Venus, the goddess of beauty. However, other pioneers in the area must not have been as well versed in Roman goddesses and thought the town was named Venice, which is what stuck. The name Ross came about from the U.S. Post Office's designation of the post office as Ross, for Ross Township, which was created in 1834. The name Ross eventually became more prominent because people were tired of their mail being sent to Erie County's Venice, Ohio, and receiving it a week late.

Dr. Clark practiced medicine in the area until his death in 1826. Venice also had another doctor practicing at the time. Dr. John Wood had moved to the area from New York in 1816 and stayed until 1826, when he moved to Illinois. Dr. Wood also ran a tavern in Venice. It was located at the main crossroads in the center of town. The main road through the early village was the road from Lawrenceburg, Indiana, to Columbus, Ohio. Once the bridge was constructed, it paved the way for the Colerain Pike. Layhigh Road is the third road in this extended five-way intersection. In the early days, taverns usually served as stops and places for travelers to spend the night, and hotels remained a mainstay at these crossroads for many decades.

Frank Ochs was a local farmer and eventually ran one of these hotels from the late 1800s until the early 1900s, when tragedy struck. The site where Ochs Tavern stood (it was known as Ochs Tavern for years, then as the Ochs Hotel) was on the same plot of land where Woods had his building. On August 16, 1909, the hotel was engulfed in flames. In the building at the time was the widow, Mrs. Ochs, who had lost her husband a year prior; a Mr. James Brant, his wife and five children; and, it was believed, Mr. and Mrs. Frank Beaver, who also ran an ice cream business in the hotel building. The fire had actually started in that ice cream parlor and created a dangerous situation when rescuers came to the aid of the eighty-one-year-old widow and the Brandt family. Many nearby buildings were endangered by the blaze. It threatened the entire town. The bucket brigade was successful, and there was no loss of life, but the Ochs Hotel was no more.

When the fire marshal investigated the cause of the fire, he became suspicious, and the ice cream man and his wife were held at the police station in Hamilton. Beaver was charged on the nineteenth with setting the fire in his ice cream establishment. It was believed he did it to claim the $1,300 in insurance money. It was said in the papers that Beaver acted strange the night of the fire. He didn't offer to help the fire brigade, and neither he nor his wife attempted to save any of their belongings; it was said that Mr. Beaver just stood by and watched it burn. Originally, he was released because all the evidence was circumstantial; however, he then was brought to trial on November 19. He was found guilty a few days later. On November 26, he was found dead in his cell. He had borrowed a razor from another inmate and given himself a very close shave. In a letter he left to his wife, he wrote that he could "not stand the disgrace of being arrested." More than one medium has spoken about feelings of a suicide in the building. While nothing has shown up during research related to specific on-site suicides, perhaps they were connected to the spirit of Mr. Beaver?

One medium also experienced multiple feelings related to medical incidents, sicknesses (possibly epidemics) and seeing a doctor. Epidemics did occur in the mid-1800s—cholera struck Ohio a few times—so that isn't a surprise. Dr. Wood did practice medicine on the site. Another connection the mediums felt was a blacksmith, and there was a blacksmith located there during the time of Dr. Wood's ownership of the lot.

After the destruction of the Ochs Hotel, the land was purchased by the Schradins, and a new chapter of the Venice/Ross community began. Stanley Schradin officially announced the name of his great endeavor in February 1918: the Venice Pavilion. Opening day was set for July 4, 1918. It was a large building that housed bowling lanes, billiards and even target shooting on the basement floor. The main floor was well known as the place to get the Pavilion's popular chicken dinners. There was also a large bar with a soda fountain, ice cream and candy for the children and a tobacco shop for the men. The upper floor was used for affairs including dancing, parties, community events and meetings. It was the social center of the village.

In 1946, Paul and Dorothy Fiehrer purchased the Venice Pavilion, and under them, it became such a popular place in the Tri-State Area that there were nights where people had to be turned away. They drew live acts such as the Carter Family (with June Carter, future wife of Johnny Cash), country music legend Tex Ritter (father of actor John Ritter) and many others.

Another perception a medium reported in the building was a strong religious feeling. Specifically, there was a strong sensation of the Catholic

The Venice Pavilion in 1919, within a year of its opening. *Lane Public Library George C. Cummins "Remember When" Photograph Collection.*

The Venice Pavilion in 1942, a few years before the Fiehrers owned it. *Lane Public Library George C. Cummins "Remember When" Photograph Collection.*

Church, seeing rosaries and other Catholic items. He said it felt lovely and special; it was a refreshing, soothing energy. He even asked if there was a Catholic church or shrine nearby. There isn't, but the Fiehrers are a Catholic family, and Paul had been a star athlete at Hamilton Catholic High. The kids and grandkids attended the local Catholic schools, as do some of his great-grandkids today. It seems that they left some of that energy in the Pavilion.

While the Fiehrer family ran and lived in the Venice Pavilion, they had no encounters that they would have said were supernatural. However, there was one exceptionally scary event on July 31, 1957, that turned the town into an inferno. A man driving a car ran a red light and collided with a gasoline truck, and the spilled gasoline was ignited by sparks from a downed wire, spreading flames everywhere. An eighteen-year-old man, Tom Burns, gave his account of the accident to the *Cincinnati Enquirer*:

> *I was just going in the door of the Venice Pavilion, and I heard a terrific crash. I looked back and saw a car and gasoline truck on their sides. A woman was trying to get out of the car. Suddenly sparks from a wire set the leaking gasoline on fire and the woman was swallowed by the flames.*

However, according to officials, there was no woman, and Burns was not the only one to have said they saw a woman trying to get out of the car only to be consumed by flames. The only actual reported death was that of the man who was driving the car. Butler County coroner Garret Boone said that even though multiple people reported a woman in the automobile, there was "very likely" only one person in the vehicle. He went on to say that the man may have had some of his wife's clothes in the car and "this would account for the reports that a woman was in the vehicle." It seems an extremely strange tale. Multiple buildings and cars were destroyed; the Venice Pavilion and another home reported damage. The first time the medium came to the Pavilion, he arrived late; he said an old woman kept trying to prevent him from reaching his destination while he was driving there. He did not elaborate as to how she was doing this, but could this have been the spirit of the immolated woman?

That tragedy wasn't the only one to happen during the tenure of the Fiehrers' ownership. Two people were killed in an incident in July 1974; one of the dead was a waitress at the establishment. Robert Burns entered the Venice Pavilion after being arrested earlier for disorderly conduct, which involved him throwing a glass at a Pavilion employee. When he returned,

Aftermath of the July 31, 1957 devastation in front of the Venice Pavilion, after a car crashed into a tanker truck. *Lane Public Library George C. Cummins "Remember When" Photograph Collection.*

he was refused service, and an altercation broke out. Dorothy Grubb, who was finished with her shift at the Pavilion, was enjoying a drink with friends when Burns tried to go behind the bar. Grubbs was seated at the bar along with James Holbert and Harold Baker, and he and Holbert tried to prevent Burns from getting behind the bar. Baker yelled at him to stop, and Burns

The wreckage of the tanker truck and the car involved in the July 31, 1957 inferno. *Lane Public Library George C. Cummins "Remember When" Photograph Collection.*

went for Baker. In the ensuing melee, Grubbs was accidentally shot in the abdomen, and Holbert and Burns were also injured, with Burns being shot in the chest, abdomen and arm. Burns later died of his injuries at Mercy Hospital in Hamilton. Baker was arrested in connection with the shootings, charged with negligent homicide for the death of Burns and acquitted in the death of Grubb. His sentence was suspended.

Mediums have mentioned sensing former employees in the Pavilion, especially a woman in the stairway. Other people, including some vendors, have encountered a woman, believed to be a former employee, on the stairs to the second floor. One woman claimed she was almost knocked down by an invisible force that seemed to be walking down the stairs she was walking up. The bar, with its large, mirrored backdrop, remains in the antique mall and was the location of a peculiar photograph taken by Jana Emmons, the granddaughter of Paul Fiehrer. Members of the Fiehrer family still visit the Venice Pavilion to reminisce about their life there. When Jana took a photo with the bar in the background, an extra person was seen in the mirror. That is to say, they only appeared in the mirror's reflection; where there should have been the person casting the reflection in the mirror, there simply wasn't anyone or anything. The person looked like a man wearing a hat. Sadly, the photo was lost. These chance encounters do make one wonder if they are connected to that night—or were they just remnants of guests and employees from another night at the Pavilion?

After the passing of Paul Fiehrer and forty years of ownership, the building closed its doors as a restaurant, showplace and community gathering spot. Rumors circulated that it might be torn down and replaced with a convenience store. When Ross native Dottie Grome heard that might happen, she purchased the building and began restoring it.

With the Venice Pavilion becoming an antique mall, through the ownership of Dottie Grome and now Jana Harmon, it has become a gathering place of many historic objects as old as Native American relics to articles from twentieth-century wars. Aside from the rich history of the Pavilion and the land it is on, the building has accumulated old objects, which can bring along spirits that were attached to them in life. Paranormal investigators have picked up an audio recording of a spirit saying the name Emily, and other folks have said they've seen a woman in older, possibly 1800s-era, attire. It is hard to determine the origins of these spirits, as they could be tied to the land or the building—or they could be transitory specters that leave when items are sold.

One particular item was definitely known to have had a spirit attached. A vendor who specialized in World War II paraphernalia had a Nazi uniform jacket hanging in his booth. Jana relayed a story about a medium who picked up something—or, more precisely, someone—from the coat, and due to the fact that there were two German-speaking people at the Pavilion, they were able to have a short conversation with the spirit attached to the jacket. Jana could not recall what was actually said, but the medium would relay the questions and answers back and forth, without knowing German, by using the German speakers to translate what the man was telling her.

The Venice Pavilion may not offer dancing and chicken dinners anymore, but it still has a lot to offer. Its three floors of antiques from numerous vendors have something for everyone, and maybe you'll even experience a spirit or two. Hours and other information can be found on its Facebook page.

Municipal Hauntings

The Art Deco–style building was built under the U.S. government's Public Works Administration. Today, the building is named the Frederick G. Mueller Building for the Hamilton architect who designed it. The building opened on November 25, 1935. The building had a fire station, council chambers, courtrooms and a jail.

The building also houses Jennifer Douglas's Angelic Crystal Therapy shop. When she first moved into the building, she felt the presence of "low vibrational entities" in the office space. A former business partner said she heard what sounded like an interrogation and screams in another part of the building. Others claim to have heard footsteps in the empty hallways. The old jail cells still exist on the upper floors. Could these darker spirits have been brought in by criminals who were imprisoned here?

Hamilton's glory days of producing legal alcohol for consumption ended in 1941 with the closure of Martin Mason's Eagle Brewery. Even though brewing came back to Butler County with the opening of the Miller plant in 1991, it returned to Hamilton with Municipal Brew Works' 2016 opening in the municipal building's former Hamilton Fire Department Station No. 2. They have had strange occurrences since the first day. On opening day, friends of Laura Goodman—the wife of Jim Goodman, one of the brewery owners—took a group selfie in front of the building. The women unexpectedly found what looked like another person in their photo with them. It is "off"—it's transparent, blurry—but you can see the facial structure, although not in detail. A couple months later, a man came into the brewery; his grandfather had worked as a dispatcher in the station. The photo was brought up because there was a resemblance between the man and the blurred face from the photo. When Jim and Laura showed the photo to him, he thought for sure it was his grandfather "Dutch," a dispatcher who had passed away in the building from a heart attack.

Municipal building at night, 1950s. *Lane Public Library, Joseph A. Cella Digital Photograph Collection.*

About three weeks after the brewery's opening, another owner, Dave Frey, was closing up for the night. There were still a few patrons finishing up in the taproom. While he was cleaning near the men's restroom, he saw a shadow pass behind him as someone entered the restroom. The four guests left, and he realized that no one had ever exited the restroom. The men's restrooms are located where the assistant fire chief's office used to be. In 1971, the assistant chief sent a team of five firefighters to assist with a blaze in Oxford. Only four returned. Once the story about the shadow seen entering the former assistant chief's office made the rounds, former firefighters came to believe it was the deceased fireman returning to share his final report. One thing that is even stranger is that this firefighter's presence has also been felt at another former Hamilton fire station.

Company No. 7 Firehouse located on Shuler Avenue may have been closed in 2013, but has a former employee decided to stay around? *Author's collection.*

The Old Company No. 7 Firehouse, built in 1910, located on Schuler Avenue in Hamilton, is said to be haunted, possibly by the same spirit. On the morning of August 5, 1971, a fire broke out in downtown Oxford. Aid from all over the county was called to assist in fighting the blaze. That afternoon, four men were fighting the fire when the front façade began to buckle. Amazingly, a picture in the August 11, 1971 *Journal News* shows deputy fire chief Stanley Meyer running toward the men to warn them as the building collapsed. Meyer was the only one killed.

Firefighters from the old station said they would hear footsteps and other incidents in the building that made them believe Meyer was still keeping an eye on things around the building.

Hose towers were a requirement in older firehouses, so the hoses could be hung to dry. The modern firehose doesn't require drying, so the hose tower has become a relic of the past. The station in the Hamilton Municipal Building had a hose tower, although it was in the building interior, and it stretched approximately thirty feet to the basement. There was a catwalk on the second floor for the firemen to reach and move the hoses as required to dry them. During the construction of the brewery, the catwalk needed to be removed. Three weeks after opening, the pendant light that hung where the catwalk used to be started swinging. None of the other lights did, and it wasn't a little bit of movement—it was making a wide path in its arc. They have never had that happen again, and they do have that on video. Jim Goodman said that they heard from a former fireman that one of the firemen would take naps on the catwalk. Could he have been upset that his favorite place for catnaps was removed?

Since the brewery stood in the same location as the former Hamilton Fire Station No. 2, the brewers decided to honor the station by naming a beer after it. Their rye pale ale was dubbed Station 2. As Jim explained,

> We mill our grains for each batch, and then they are conveyed to our grist cast, which then holds the milled grain and drops them into our mash tun. The auger which transfers the grain from the mill to the grist case has a safety switch which turns off the mill if the path were to get congested. The first time we ever brewed "Station 2," the safety switch failed and ended up snapping the industrial-strength heavy-gauge aluminum sprocket responsible for transferring the grain. It is something that seemed impossible to have happened, with the safety switch malfunctioning, then the heavy-gauge sprocket snapping. It's never happened on previous beers brewed or any since and just coincidentally happened during the process of making the beer named for the former fire station.

About a month and a half after opening, Jim went in to pick up some kegs to take to a customer. As he entered the building that morning, he heard something a brewer never wants to hear: liquid splashing on concrete. Then he noticed a stream going under the bar to the floor drain. The tank's valve was open and leaking the fire station's namesake beer, Station 2. Jim called the head brewer, who was the last to leave the previous night, and told him what he found. Of course, the head brewer was dumbfounded by what had happened; of all people, he would have noticed—and especially heard—if the beer was leaking out before he left. After all, it was his work literally going down the drain. They lost sixteen barrels of beer that morning. It seems as if maybe one of the spirits is (or was) a teetotaler and not a fan of alcohol—especially when it is named for the station. Maybe that's because firefighting is such a dangerous job that the spirits of the firefighters don't like being tempted to drink at the station? It seems that a lot of the activity started shortly after opening, and it's common to hear about paranormal activity when construction and changes are going on in a space. When you also have the added excitement and energy of a brewery opening, there is the possibility of stirring something up—plus, as has been mentioned, other spirits from the building could be making themselves at home. Employees still have some experiences—some have even claimed they were touched—so you may want to stop by, grab a beer (Orange Agave Blonde is my personal favorite) and ask your friendly server if they have had any experiences.

CHAPTER 6

TRAVELING SPIRITS

THE OXFORD GHOST LIGHT

Almost everyone in southwestern Ohio knows about the legend of the Oxford Ghost Light. The legend itself has many variations. The basic story is that you park facing south on Oxford-Milford Road at Earhart Road at the ninety-degree turn, turn off your car, then flash your lights three times. You will see a white light heading north on Oxford-Milford Road, coming toward you. This is the ghost of a motorcycle rider who has a tragic story, a story that comes in many forms—some slightly changed, others with a little more detail, some very different, but they all have the same ending. What seems to be the original story is said to have taken place after World War II. A returning soldier was on his way to surprise his girlfriend. He saw a rival's car in the driveway and, enraged, he accidentally missed the turn, hitting a barbed-wire fence. The metal wire tore through his flesh and vertebrae like a hot knife through butter, his head flying in one direction and the bike, with a headless rider, in another. One variation adds a tearjerker, saying that the soldier was on his way to propose.

Over the years, the story began to take on many forms. There are the farmer's daughter versions, where the biker would ride back and forth at all hours of the night after being forbidden to see his girlfriend. The girlfriend's father, a farmer, strung wire across the road, which beheaded the biker. A twist on this version has the couple both getting beheaded by the barbed wire and the distraught farmer killing himself over the guilt. Some other versions end with the death of the girlfriend, who, distraught over her boyfriend's death, hanged herself in a barn. This *Romeo and Juliet* ending was also added onto other retellings.

The headlight flashes to signal the biker had no part in the early stories, but elements to give a reason for them were added in later versions. One version says that the girlfriend on Earhart Road was dating a young man, and her parents did not approve of him. They forbade her from seeing him. She devised a way to signal the biker that her parents were asleep by flashing the front porch light (or her bedroom light) three times. The boyfriend would be on Oxford-Milford Road, waiting. On seeing the lights flash, he would ride up to Earhart Road, pick up his waiting girlfriend and have her back before her parents knew she was gone. Well, you know how it ends. Sometimes drinking is said to have played a part.

Some versions of the story actually said to park at the farmhouse and then flash your lights three times, summoning the ghost rider by mimicking the porch light signal. The most drastic retelling adds the element of danger to the girlfriend. This one comes from the days of the "Oxford Rapist/ Strangler," depending on who is telling the story. In the first version, the girl was all alone in her house on Earhart Road. A strange car pulled up, and the driver began honking the horn and flashing the lights. The car matched the description of the vehicle driven by the Oxford Rapist. In a panic, she called her boyfriend, who hopped on his motorcycle and, in a rush, missed the turn. The alternate version of the story has the girl home alone for the night. She told her boyfriend, who lived around the bend on Oxford-Milford Road, that she was scared to be home alone with the rapist on the loose. He told her if she got suspicious of anything to flash her porch lights and he'd be right over. Well, the Oxford Rapist chose that night to try to break into her house. The girlfriend frantically flashed her porch lights, her boyfriend saw the flashing lights and sped off on his motorcycle—and yet again, the ninety-degree turn, the barbed-wire fence and the missing head.

In another story involving the lights, it was dark and raining very hard. A farmer on a tractor heading south on Oxford-Milford Road flashed his lights to warn the motorcyclist of the sharp ninety-degree turn. The biker ignored the warning, losing his head at the fence.

Some versions of the story also involve seeing a red light after the white light. This light has a few backstories as well. Some accounts say that it is the red lights of the ambulance going to the accident site. Likewise, you may see the ghost of the girlfriend running toward the accident site. Sometimes it's a car that makes the turn off Earhart and catches the rider off guard; he swerves and is decapitated once again. In this story, the red taillights that are seen are the rear lights of the car. One version is that a bicyclist pulled out in front of the motorcycle rider, causing him to swerve and hit the fence. In some versions, the bicycle rider dies also. The red lights that are seen are the red reflectors on the bicycle. Still another version has the red lights being the motorcycle taillights. As the ghost rider approaches you, he realizes the flashing lights are not his girlfriend, and he turns around and heads back south on Oxford-Milford Road.

As far as the light itself, there are stories that the light will follow you home after you see it. Another says that if the light reaches your car, you will die. I even heard one story about a friend of a friend who had the light go through their car, cracking the windshield. Many people throughout the years have seen a single light traveling northbound on Oxford-Milford Road. It is typically described as white or bluish-white and very bright. The questions remain: How did the story start, and is there any history behind a horrible death at the ninety-degree turn?

Looking south on Oxford-Milford Road at Earhart Road, where the mysterious ghost light has supposedly been seen for years. *Author's collection.*

There are many ghost light stories all across the world. The Oxford Light shares many similarities with another Ohio ghost light story, that of the Elmore Rider, near Elmore, Ohio. This story has a young man returning from the Great War. The first thing he wanted to do was propose to the girlfriend he left. He went to her door, planning to surprise her. Unfortunately, he was the one surprised. She was with another man. She said she was married while he was gone. In a fit of anger and sadness, he ran out, jumped on his motorcycle and sped off. He missed the turn near the bridge and wrecked. His head was torn from his body by a barbed-wire fence. The date was March 21. If you go to this bridge in Sandusky County on that date, flash your lights and honk your horn three times, you will see the motorcycle headlight come from the house, travel up the road and vanish at the bridge, following the route of his last ride.

You can see the great many similarities between the stories of the Elmore and the Oxford ghost lights.

The Elmore light had a run of articles in the local papers in the summer and fall of 1922, with a vastly different origin. In the 1922 version, the light travels the route in reverse. It starts at the bridge, then goes to a house that is haunted by a man who hanged himself. Theories about the Elmore Ghost Light abounded, from phosphorous gas to reflection and refraction of headlights to pranksters. One man mentioned seeing the light in the area as a child in the 1860s. The man and his family would watch it travel for miles from his farm. He said after seeing all the recent articles about the Elmore Rider, he wanted to let the younger generation know that the light had been around for a long time. The story of the Elmore Rider rose in popularity when folklorist Richard Gill began investigating the phenomenon of the light in 1968. He wrote about it in the *Ohio Folklore Society Journal* in December 1972.

On October 31, 1992, the *Hamilton Journal News* published an interview with seventy-year-old William Falk, who lived in the old farmhouse where the girlfriend supposedly resided. He said he was actually born in and lived in that house his entire life. He went on to say that he knew nothing of the story and believed the light was not a ghost. He said the "ghost light" was nothing but airplane lights and bright stars. He also said he had been robbed multiple times and was constantly bothered by trespassing thrill seekers.

There have been no verified reports of any deadly motorcycle accidents at the intersection of Oxford-Milford and Earhart Roads. However, State Route 73 east of Oxford was a deadly stretch of road in the mid-1960s.

From August 1965 to March 1966, there were eight fatalities. The hilly four-mile section of road east of Oxford was nicknamed the Death Strip, and the hills were referred to as the Death Humps. Governor James A. Rhodes ordered the highway department to "get rid of the humps," and patrols were increased in the area to stop speeding and illegal passing until construction was finished along the deadly section of road.

There has been no record of an "Oxford Rapist" or an "Oxford Strangler." However, there was a serial killer known as the Cincinnati Strangler who was believed to have murdered seven women between December 1965 and December 1966. Although all his rapes and murders were of women in the city of Cincinnati, the terror extended across the Tri-State region.

The bicyclist story is more commonly set on nearby Buckley Road. This story seems to have appeared in the '90s. It's believed to have started one of two ways. One is by accident; someone just got the roads wrong, college kids mistaking one dark, creepy road for another. The other theory behind the Buckley Road story is that with increased police presence at Oxford-Milford Road, due to neighbor complaints, people started going out to this road. Sometimes you just want an excuse to park in the dark with your date, and one ghost story is as good as another, especially if there's a lesser chance of running into a Butler County sheriff.

As far as my research goes, the Oxford Ghost Light stories have been around since the late 1960s. The Elmore Ghost Rider story was well known since before the 1920s and attracted increased interest in the late 1960s. Ever since I read the Elmore story in Chris Woodyard's *Haunted Ohio*, I have believed the Oxford story probably originated from the Elmore tale. It may have been brought to Oxford by a Miami University student from northern Ohio who was familiar with the story of the Elmore Ghost Rider. A student could bring a ghost story with him, but how could he bring a ghost light? One explanation may be where farmer Josephus Burns and his horrid discovery come in.

It was March 25, 1945, when farmer Burns discovered the remains of a woman in a ravine while chasing a runaway pig on his property along Harker's Run. The coroner declared it an act of murder. Now they had to figure out who she was and who killed her. There had been hard spring rains in the days leading up to the discovery of the corpse, so any evidence left by the killer was washed away. The unknown woman had been dead at least a week. The coroner's report showed that there were severe bruises on the neck and three stab wounds to the head. According to a March 26 *Dayton Herald* article, the deceased was "between 30 and 35 years old, five feet eight inches tall, weighing about 135 pounds with light brown hair and brown eyes." The sheriff's office had nothing else to go on. Luckily, they caught a mysterious break. An unidentified female caller phoned the Hamilton police headquarters on March 26. According to a June 23, 1946, *New York Daily News* article, the caller stated that a check should be made "on the whereabouts of Mrs. Nellie Tuttle of 421 North Seventh Street. I think she may have been murdered."

The detective who received the call was Robert Dinwiddie. He posed as a door-to-door insurance salesman in the neighborhood in an attempt to get information out of the neighbors. All the stories he received were the same: a week ago, Mrs. Tuttle left her husband for another man. Then he spoke to the neighbors who lived behind the Tuttles. Mrs. Martha Hubbard said she hoped Nellie Tuttle did leave with another man because of the way her husband, Elton Tuttle, had treated her. The Sunday before her disappearance, Ms. Tuttle ran into the Hubbard's home and said her husband was chasing her with a kitchen knife.

Detective Dinwiddie also found out that right after his wife's disappearance, Elton Tuttle bought a used car—suspiciously, the first car he ever owned. Dinwiddie followed up with Nellie's foster parents, the Whites, who lived in Sharonville. The Whites were asked to view the body and identified it as the little girl they raised. "That's our poor Nellie," said Mr. White.

Immediately, the police went to bring in Mr. Tuttle. He was under police interrogation for seven hours, never answering any questions. The police then took him to the morgue. According to the *New York Daily News*, his confession unfolded as his eyes fell on the once-beautiful face of his wife. He stared and tearfully mumbled, "I did it," followed by a loud cry: "Get me out of here!"

Elton Tuttle told the police that when she returned home the night of the twelfth, they got into a familiar quarrel. He was angry that she always chose having fun over taking care of their two sons. He believed she was with another man. She said she would kill herself and the boys if he tried to leave her. The two boys slept soundly upstairs as the arguing reached a fever pitch, until Elton grabbed a hand axe and swung, hitting his wife in the head three times.

As he stood over the body, with blood pooling on the kitchen floor, he knew he had to cover up the murder and remove any connections to him. He hid the body in the basement. Then he cleaned the blood from the kitchen and went to bed. The next morning, he fixed the children breakfast and took them to a nursery, then he went to work. He followed his regular schedule the rest of the week. Tuttle arranged to purchase a used vehicle and took the boys to spend the weekend with their grandparents in Kentucky. Elton burned the axe handle in the stove and threw the axe head into the Great Miami River. He methodically removed any labels from his wife's clothing. Around midnight the following day, he placed the body in the car and sped away. On returning, he knew he had to spread a story of his wife's infidelity to the neighbors. Everything went as planned—until that mysterious phone call.

Elton Tuttle went to trial on July 18, 1945, for second-degree murder, because the prosecutor knew premeditation could not be proved. Tuttle told the jury of the infidelity, letters between her and soldiers; he said she left him and the children alone for twenty-three nights straight. After hearing his story, the eight women and four men on the jury reduced the crime even more, and he was sentenced to only first-degree manslaughter, carrying a mandatory sentence of one to twenty years. He died at sixty-eight in Florida on May 28, 1983, and was buried near his parents in Kentucky.

How exactly does this tie into the Oxford Ghost Light? When Elton Tuttle left his house that night with the corpse of his wife, he headed out toward Oxford. He knew of a ravine where he could throw the body—a place that was remote and, with some luck, would probably never be found. Even if the body was found, it would take a long time, allowing it to rot and become unidentifiable—or so he thought. As Tuttle drove out of town on Hamilton-Richmond Road, he passed through Darrtown and turned left on Oxford-Trenton Road (SR 73). He continued to travel west, then turned right onto Oxford-Milford Road, traveling north, and he pulled over where a ravine comes closest to the road, right as the road makes a ninety-degree turn. He removed the body from the car on the dark, empty, desolate road. Then carried it over to the edge and hurled it over the fifty-foot drop. He heard the breaking of branches and rocks and gravel sliding down the ravine, then all was silent. The location where the body of Nellie Tuttle was discarded, the land owned by the farmer Josephus Burns, is where you park your car to summon the ghost light, and that light follows the path that Elton Tuttle drove to eliminate the evidence of the murder. Is it the spirit of Nellie Tuttle following the road to the location of her unceremonious abandonment, or is it just a coincidence?

Others think that the ghost light goes back even further. The 1992 *Hamilton Journal News* article also quotes a resident who believes the light may originate with disturbed Native American burial grounds behind his property on Oxford-Milford Road. This seems plausible to me, because I heard something in the woods when I visited the light decades ago, a rhythmic drumbeat that got louder but never very loud. The 1914 *Ohio Archeological Atlas* shows a series of mounds along the western side of Harker's Run, one directly across the ravine from the bend. We have seen stories about ghost lights associated with Native American sites; is this another?

Others believe it's all just an optical illusion. There are many peaks, valleys, driveways and side roads all along the Oxford-Milford Road. Is it simply the headlights of cars turning into driveways or side roads? People have also said that the light seems very bright. If your eyes have adjusted to the dark and then you see a bright light, it would disrupt your night vision, making it appear brighter. Whether it's the spirit of Nellie Tuttle, Native American spirits, optical illusions or a headless motorcycle rider, the only thing we do know for certain is that there is a mysterious light on Oxford-Milford Road.

THE MOANING BRIDGE OF HAMILTON

In the latter half of the nineteenth century, the reservoirs along the hydraulic canal were used to harvest ice in the winter and for pleasure boating in the summer. The Hamilton Club House rented out rowboats at the head of the large reservoir. The canal itself was crossed by numerous low wooden bridges, and the boaters would have to duck as they passed under.

An October 20, 1889 *Cincinnati Enquirer* article claimed this event happened a few years prior. A young couple frequented the reservoir, boating along the canal and enjoying their time together. Friends waited for the engagement to be announced, because they knew it was imminent. However, before the young man could propose, he found out he had consumption and didn't have much time left. He also didn't want to make his beautiful young lady a young widow. One day, he paddled them toward the far north end of the canal, away from the reservoir, where he knew they wouldn't be bothered. In a selfish turn, the young lover had decided if he couldn't have her in marriage, he would have her in eternity. He pulled a gun out, shot her in the head, then turned the gun on himself. Her body slumped over the boat, blood running through her blond curls into the water, leaving a red streak in the flowing canal as the boat drifted downstream, snagging on some debris under one of the low bridges. About

Boating on the reservoir was a fun summer activity for folks, as this 1895 photograph shows—although not all boating trips ended happily. *Lane Public Library George C. Cummins "Remember When" Photograph Collection.*

that time, a farmer came upon the bridge. As he crossed the bridge, he heard what he initially thought was a woman moaning from beneath it. He got down and strained to look underneath. He couldn't see anything and figured it must have just been the old bridge creaking.

The next day, the workers at the Hamilton Club House were greeted with an eerie sight. One of their boats had floated along through the night, leaving a dark red streak in the water. In the boat was the dead young man and his dead young partner. She had apparently survived the initial shot but passed away in the night. Some of the stories from that period include hearing the moans at the bridge, seeing streaks of blood in the water between the bridge and the clubhouse and even seeing the ghostly rowboat. There still are some bridges crossing the old canal; one of them is a new pedestrian bridge that is easily accessible. The others are on private land. It's not known if any moaning is heard on warm summer nights near any of these bridges.

THE GHOSTS OF MAUD-HUGHES ROAD

It was a decades-old rite of passage for many Butler County teens: traveling out the dark, tree-lined road to the bridge. Maud-Hughes Road runs along the western side of the train tracks from Princeton Road, and at the bridge, it crosses over to follow the east side to Millikin Road. That bridge was called the Screaming Bridge of Maud-Hughes Road. The road made a backward *S* shape at the bridge. An old superstition used to say that bridges were made that way to confuse the devil. In reality, it was just easier back in those days to build a bridge perpendicular to the crossing instead of at an awkward angle. In 2014, the bridge was closed, torn down and replaced. The sharp ninety-degree turns leading to the bridge at either end were smoothed out; now the bridge angles over the tracks instead of being perpendicular. There were many stories associated with that bridge; not many know that the first ghostly screams originated near a smaller bridge to the north.

The site of the earliest hauntings along these tracks is near the Kyle's Station Road crossing. The Kyle's Station community grew up around a train station built on land owned by Thomas Kyle, who settled the land in

Deaths when the road and railroad were at the same grade at Kyle's Station may have given rise to the tales of Butler County's first screaming bridge. *Author's collection.*

1803. Maud-Hughes Road travels up to Kyle's Station Road on the east side of the tracks, jogs under this train overpass and continues north on the west side of the tracks. Originally, the crossing was at grade and was the scene of many deaths and injuries.

What is believed to be the story that gave rise to the Kyles Station haunting happened on April 5, 1898, when three itinerant workers from Madison County were in the area searching for jobs on the rail line. Lewis DeLong; his nineteen-year-old wife, Melissa; and Melissa's sister found an abandoned cabin on the Scudder Farm near Kyles Station to spend the night. Lewis got a fire going, and the threesome lay down near the hearth planning for a warm night's rest. Fate had other plans. Lewis and his sister-in-law were awakened by the shrill screams of Melissa. A spark from the fire had landed on her dress, igniting it. The natural fiber dress burned quickly and fought efforts to be put out. By the time they got the fire extinguished, Melissa DeLong was dead. The *Journal News* and the *Dayton Daily News* both stated that she was "burnt to a crisp." Her screams were heard in the area for years after.

There have been other ghost stories along these rails. People have told stories of a train engineer who died in an accident and walks the rails near Kyle's Station carrying a light. He may be the same ghost behind the legend of the Milliken Light, another ghostly light that has been seen on the tracks near Milliken Road.

The story of the Screaming Bridge of Maud-Hughes Road was the generic "Crybaby Bridge" story. Ohio itself has its fair share. The story is that an unwed mother threw her baby over a bridge. In most versions, the mother followed. The screams are the mother, the baby or both. Usually, it's a bridge over water, but in this instance, it is a bridge over train tracks. One version has the mother hanging herself from the bridge. If you did the ritual of flashing your lights or honking your horn three times, you'd see the girl hanging. This makes no sense, because she hanged herself from the bridge, and you're parked on the bridge. Another story involved two lovers who decided to get into a little hanky-panky under the bridge and didn't hear the train. Both of these stories are the typical kind told to act as a warning to young adults that premarital sex is bad.

Screams from the bridge aren't the only strange happenings around the bridge. Red lights from a ghostly caboose have been seen. There is a train that appears normal, but as it approaches the Maud-Hughes Bridge, it simply vanishes. People have also had the experience of seeing a person walking along Maud-Hughes Road who also just disappears. There have

Railroad accidents set the stage for future ghost stories in Butler County. This photo shows the aftermath of two trains that collided on the Cincinnati, Hamilton & Dayton Railroad. *MidPointe Library System, George C. Crout Collection.*

also been reports of ghostly mists and hooded figures. During the late '80s and early '90s era of Satanic Panic, it was said devil worshippers hung out in the area. Spray-painted pentagrams and satanic graffiti adorned the concrete structure under the bridge.

Many people cite a 1909 explosion on the railroad tracks as a source for the ghost train. A leaky boiler in an engine exploded, killing two and seriously injuring three others in the engine. It could make the basis for a ghost story, except that the explosion occurred five and a half miles south.

There were many accidents on the line near there, but none were fatal until after the ghost stories began. On the night of Friday 17, 1972, three Lakota students, ages thirteen, fourteen and fifteen, were hit and killed by an oncoming train. On the early morning of June 8, 1976, near the intersection of Princeton Road and Maud-Hughes Road, two trains collided, killing one person. In February 1985, a planned fight at the bridge between Lakota students ended in an accidental shooting death.

Maud-Hughes Road was known to have been a popular hangout for high school kids for decades. It was known as a lover's lane in the late '60s, if not earlier, and there is one horrific incident that could have turned the lover's lane into the screaming bridge.

On the afternoon of Sunday, October 18, 1970, two men were horseback riding along Gregory Creek, which runs under Princeton Pike and along Maud-Hughes Road. They saw something along the creek, and as they got closer, they realized it was the naked, mutilated body of a girl. The newspapers described the site as a "tree-lined lover's lane"; now it looked like a scene from a horror movie. The victim had been shot in the left temple; a deep gash ran from her left shoulder to her right thigh; a letter Z was carved into her stomach. There were worse mutilations that I will not expand on here, but they attracted the FBI.

The next day, the mother of sixteen-year-old Cheryl Segal received a phone call from her daughter's friend, Karen. She asked if Cheryl got home safe the night before. Cheryl never arrived home. The girls had received a ride home from the friend of a friend, twenty-nine-year-old James Findley. The girls were uneasy, but Cheryl was tired. Karen was dropped off first and tried to get Cheryl to stay with her, but Cheryl just wanted to go home. On hearing Karen's story, Cheryl's mother immediately called the police. Her daughter's remains were found around four o'clock that afternoon. The police put out an APB on Findley, and he was taken into custody around nine thirty on Monday morning and charged with first-degree murder.

On Monday, January 26, 1971, Findley was charged with murder and faced the death penalty. His alibi was that on his way to take Cheryl home, he stopped by his own house and decided he wanted to stay there with his wife, and his brother-in-law took the girl home. On February 1, 1971, James Findley was sentenced to die, with no mercy, in Ohio's electric chair. Findley stated, "You are going to know I am not guilty…when you get the next one." Ultimately, Findley was given a stay of execution pending his appeal and then a permanent stay of execution when the U.S. Supreme Court ruled that certain death penalty cases were deemed unconstitutional.

The FBI took an interest in the case of Cheryl Segal because two cases in San Francisco from August 1970 involved, according to FBI records, "mutilations similar to the Ohio death." Those cases were killings by the infamous Zodiac Killer. The serial killer was known to have killed seven people in Northern California but claimed many more victims. Eventually, the investigation into Zodiac killing Cheryl was dropped, even though Findley had been in San Francisco around the time of at least one of those murders.

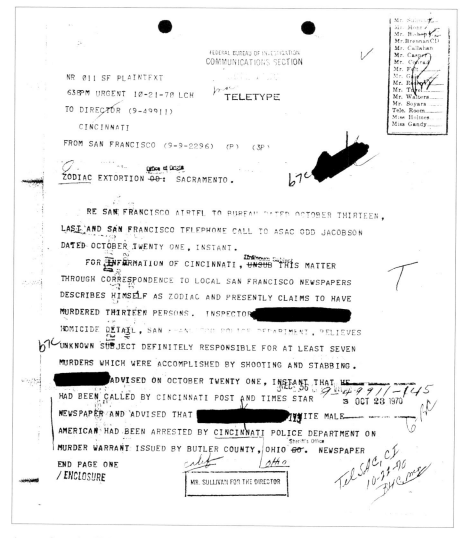

A page from the FBI's Zodiac Killer files looking into the murder that occurred near the screaming bridge of Maud-Hughes Road. *FBI Archives.*

There are many stories along this stretch of rail. There have been many deaths and many questions. Were the screams of young Cheryl heard by couples on the nearby lover's lane, and is that what gave rise to the Screaming Bridge of Maud-Hughes Road?

Amy of Lick Road

The ghost of Lick Road is another tale that has a convoluted backstory. It's not uncommon to see the name Amy spray-painted on the signs or guardrails near the end of Lick Road. Actually, no one knows who Amy was, although the most plausible connection will sound very familiar. Amy either haunts the area as a misty female form in the woods or she may write "HELP ME!" on your steamed-up windows. You may hear her walking in the woods, or you may hear her or her baby screaming and crying.

The road in and of itself has a disjointed story. It was originally called Burns Road and branched off River Road in Fairfield. It coursed its way southward along and crossed Banklick Creek, then connected to West Kemper Road. By at least 1915, the road was in service, and it had a bridge over the creek. This is known because of a 1922 *Journal News* article about a man suing the county due to timbers on the bridge giving way and causing his truck to crash. On the 1955 map, Burns Road ends after about a quarter mile and seems to become a trail along its former route until it reaches the

The bridge associated with the legend of Amy at the end of Lick Road in the Richardson Forest Preserve. *Author's collection.*

county line, where it becomes a road again, named Lick Road, in Hamilton County. Today, you can't reach the location from Butler County. The current route to the site is reached by taking Lick Road off Kemper Road in Hamilton County, then driving to where Lick Road ends, which, although part of Hamilton County's Richardson Forest Preserve, is actually just across the Butler County line. The bridge is located not too far into the woods from the end of the road.

The story is that Amy and her boyfriend were out at the end of Lick Road, either parked or on the bridge, and she was somehow killed, by accident or murder. The boyfriend left her body in the woods. Occasionally, this story is also said to have happened on their prom night. Another story is that Amy was out walking one evening and murdered while being chased into the woods. Another version involving the bridge is that Amy was waiting on her boyfriend, who never showed up, so she hanged herself. One version also includes an unwanted baby being thrown into the creek before she took her own life, the "Crybaby Bridge" trope. The story that gives us a grain of truth is that Amy was abducted and killed by a stranger and then dumped in the woods at the end of Lick Road—except in reality, her name wasn't Amy.

On August 24, 1976, a man walking his dog along Banklick Creek Road discovered the body of a fifteen-year-old girl near a small bridge over Banklick Creek. Banklick Creek Road, sometimes just called Bank Road, is also located off Kemper Road, about 1,400 feet from the intersection of Lick and Kemper Roads. The girl was found partially decomposed, with a large six-inch stab wound in her chest. Due to the fact that there was no blood in the area, it was determined she was probably murdered elsewhere and then dumped at this mostly secluded location. This location was near a wide gravel pull off where the local kids gathered to smoke and drink.

She was identified as fifteen-year-old Linda Dyer from North College Hill. The last time her parents heard from her was the night of the twenty-first. She called her parents to say she was staying with a friend. She was last seen leaving a large party in Montford Heights on the twenty-second. She was seen hitchhiking and entering an orange Volkswagen Beetle with two men inside. Her parents reported her missing on August 23 after she hadn't arrived home and they had not heard from her in two nights.

As seen from other stories, it is not uncommon for a ghost story to travel to another nearby location. How the name Amy got associated with the story is a complete unknown. There have been no records of an Amy dying or being murdered in the area. It is easy to see how this story could have been relocated from Bank Road to Lick Road. Police had been aware of teens frequently gathering in the area at night. An increased police presence probably made sitting around drinking at that location an unwise choice—especially when there was a more secluded area just over a mile away at the end of Lick Road.

The murderer of Linda Dyer was never identified. Perhaps the ghost stories are true and it's not a girl named Amy that haunts the area but a ghost named Linda at the end of Lick Road, pleading for someone to help her find her murderers so she can have peace.

THE HIGHWAY TO HEAVEN

US 27 from Ross to Oxford became known as the Highway to Heaven in the 1980s. It had been known for years to be a dangerous stretch of road. After his daughter Judy's death in December 1986, Bert Harbin erected a white cross along the side of the road where she died. That act initiated a safety campaign called the US 27 Task Force to bring attention to the deaths along that stretch of road. By March 1987, they had placed 65 white wooden crosses at the locations of accidents, with plans to erect a total of 108 crosses, one for every death from 1950 to 1987, along that sixteen-mile stretch of pavement.

People still claim to see ghostly victims of these accidents along that dangerous length of road. The drivers say they see a motorcycle in the distance, and as it gets closer, they realize it's coming right at them; at the last minute, it seems to soar over their vehicle. There have also been stories of a car coming up quickly behind the driver and tailgating them or attempting to pass them, before the phantom vehicle vanishes. The stories state no certain section of the road where the events occur, which direction you have to be driving or any other special situation in which you might see the phantom driver or rider; it's just stated as happening on US 27 between Ross and Oxford. No descriptions are given of the vehicles.

Improvements have been made to US 27 over the years, some started months after actions by the US 27 Task Force. Reflectors and flashers were put up at dangerous curves; speed limits were changed; eventually, road widenings and larger berms were added. Still, there are impatient people passing in no passing zones and speeding along stretches, and there are still accidents. As far as the ghost stories are concerned, are they actual spectral events people are experiencing, or are they meant as warnings, like Bert Harbin's white memorial crosses, reminders to drive safely, be aware and not become another statistic on the Highway to Heaven?

Coincidentally or not, as I was doing research on accidents along US 27, the first article I read was from June 1929, about a nine-year-old boy from Millville who ran out onto the road while playing with his sister. A passing car flipped over trying to avoid him, and the boy was pinned under one of the car's wheels. He received a broken arm and stitches above his left eye. That boy's name was Ralph Keller—my grandpa!

The Princeton Pike Hitchhiker

This story sounds very similar to the hitchhiker urban legend that is told in many places. The Princeton Pike story has a young woman in a prom dress hitchhiking along the road. When someone picks her up, she vanishes from the car as it passes Rose Hill Burial Park. Another bit of urban legend says that if you do not pick her up, you will have an accident. Princeton Pike was a main road into Hamilton. There are numerous articles about accidents, from runaway horse buggies to out-of-control tractor trailers. The legend has been passed down for decades and may have started with a grain of truth.

In March 1922, sheriff's deputies were left perplexed by a case. James Earhart, a county commissioner candidate, was found dead next to his car just off Princeton Pike. He was seen, with a woman in his passenger seat, shortly before his body was found. A local farmer, Otto Block, saw a woman believed to have been the same one walking along Princeton Pike, and he offered her a ride—although not to Rose Hill Burial Park, like the legends say—but she asked to be dropped off at Sixth and Sycamore Streets in Hamilton. She made no mention of Earhart, why she was walking or anything that would have clued the authorities in to her identity. Earhart's death was ruled a heart attack. The woman was never seen again. Is this strange event what gave rise to the story of the Princeton Pike Hitchhiker?

The road and area have greatly changed. What used to be a long stretch of county road is now a sea of development with shopping centers, restaurants and subdivisions almost the entire way to the county line. There hasn't been a reported sighting of the ghostly girl in decades.

CHAPTER 7
SPOOKY SCHOOLS

POASTTOWN'S HAUNT

Darrell Whisman and his wife, Brenda, purchased an empty school in 2004. They both attended the school in the 1960s. Rather than see their old school fall to the wrecking ball, like so many others, they decided to buy it. They knew they were purchasing an old building, but they didn't know what else they had received in the deal.

Poasttown may not be a familiar name to many; it lies across the Great Miami, north of Middletown. The village was laid out by Peter Post in 1818. He named it West Liberty. A post office opened in 1848, necessitating the name change from West Liberty to Post Town, named for Peter Post— eventually spelled Poast Town, then Poasttown.

The school began as a small brick building, built in 1857. It was remodeled in 1932 by the Poasttown Grange, a national group that promoted farming. The building is still there, now serving as a station house for the Madison Township Fire Department, and is located at 6415 Middletown-Germantown Road. In 1932, there were 415 students spread across seven one-room and three two-room schoolhouses in Madison Township. In 1936, a levy was passed in Madison Township for the building of a new school; the vote was 516 for to 105 against. The building opened in the fall of 1937 and was dedicated in April 1938. The celebration featured student choirs and glee clubs singing and local and state educators speaking. Decades later, after the

Poasttown School opened in 1937 and shuttered in 1999, but not everyone left. *Author's collection.*

township built a new junior high and senior high schools, the old schools, including Poasttown, were renovated to become elementary schools. Then, after sixty-three years, the school closed in 2000. The school was placed on the Ohio Historic Inventory (OHI) in 1986; the OHI report noted the building's size and placement on the site were a big change from the rest of the village, which consists of smaller buildings located up to the sidewalks, whereas the school sits back fifty yards. It is the only building of its style in the village, with columns, a large cupola, stone door surrounds and window trim. The report deemed the building unique and special to the area.

As for Darryl and Brenda, they planned to live in a portion of the building and lease out other portions. Darryl says they have also let area veterans' groups and nonprofits use the space for fundraising and charity events. The police have also been able to use the building for K-9 training and fire department practice building evacuation situations.

One thing that Darryl began noticing was the strange events he would witness when he was alone in the building. When you are in a large, abandoned building and hear locker doors slamming, hear voices and even feel people walk past you, you tend to go from a nonbeliever to a believer. After the word got out that there were strange things happening, local folks in the paranormal community reached out to offer help; this evolved into opening the building to allow groups to come in to experience things for themselves.

Research has shown the location has a possibility of being one cause of the hauntings. It may go back to prehistoric times. A Native American village, which was probably contemporary to the pioneer era, had been located on the site of the original school, according to a 1932 *Journal News* article. That site lies only about seven hundred feet away from Darryl's building. Mills's 1914 *Archeological Atlas of Ohio* also shows two Indian mounds between the railroad and Trenton-Franklin Road, where the 1937 school building resides. The land here was important to the Native people for a very long time, and that could contribute to the concentration of spirits.

Another very strong possibility is that the hauntings could stem from the worst rail disaster in Butler County, which happened near the site. On July 4, 1910, a freight train and a passenger train collided, killing twenty-four and injuring thirty-five near the site. The Cincinnati Flyer No. 21, billed as the fastest train on the New York to Cincinnati route, collided with a freight train at one o'clock in the afternoon. The tracks were covered in twisted metal and debris for one hundred yards. At that time, Middletown had no hospital, and doctors drove from Hamilton and Middletown to assist any

Spectators flock to the site of the deadly July 4, 1910 train accident near Poasttown. *MidPointe Library System, George C. Crout Collection.*

way they could. A makeshift hospital area was set up in a field south of the tracks, and the victims who were killed were laid there also. The field where the temporary morgue and hospital were set up is where the school would eventually come to be built. This wasn't the only accident on those tracks near Poasttown, either. The restless spirits inhabiting the area could be some of those whose lives were ended in an instant due to the violent and deadly train accidents.

The third possibility is that the building is haunted by the people who went to, taught and cared for the school. Many people pass through the doors of the school: students, teachers, administrative and custodial workers. It takes many to run a school. These people can leave their impression, or sometimes, they may decide to want to come back for whatever reason.

One of the saddest stories is about a young girl who, as the legend goes, fell down the stairwell and died from head injuries. From utilizing various paranormal techniques, the in-house paranormal team, POV Paranormal, came to believe her name was Sarah. They also didn't think she died in the school but instead had a head injury from her fall and died later at home. Years later, research uncovered a kindergartener from the school named Cheryl Ann Combs. She had fallen off a rocking chair on November 20, 1963, and the next day complained about her head hurting. According to the December 7 *Middletown Journal*, she was admitted to the hospital and then released before Thanksgiving and readmitted the Wednesday after. Surgery was performed on December 6, and she passed away on December 7 from swelling of the brain. Could Cheryl be the "Sarah" that people thought died from a head injury?

Daryll has some interactions that he is not very fond of speaking about. Someone or something has attacked him in the past. There is even a video of him being pulled out of bed. He's also been hit in the head and experienced other instances of something darker lurking there; these are rare occurrences, and they focus on Daryll. Many people encounter doors opening and closing, seeing shadows and hearing voices, the voices of children.

There is a webpage, www.poasttownschool.com, with much more information about the building and also links to some of the many pieces of evidence collected over the years. Poasttown School is also on Facebook, where they actively promote their paranormal events.

PEABODY'S GHOST

The most famous ghost story on Miami's campus is about the ghost of Helen Peabody. The story begins at another school, an all-female school that grew along with Miami University. The Western Female Seminary was established in 1853 and was funded by local churches and philanthropists. Modeled after the methodology of Mt. Holyoke College in Massachusetts, the Holyoke Plan, the Western Female Seminary would provide a quality education and religious teaching to young women. The Western Seminary became the first of five "daughter schools" of Mt. Holyoke.

The first building on the campus was Seminary Hall, built in 1855; it served as the dormitory and also administrative offices. The office of the principal, Helen Peabody, was also located in this building. Ms. Peabody graduated from Mt. Holyoke in 1848, and after graduation, she stayed there as a teacher until 1853. In 1855, she moved to Oxford to become the first principal of what people began to call the Mt. Holyoke of the West. The first day the school opened, Ms. Peabody welcomed each student at the door, she continued that tradition every first day of school that she was at the institution.

Just after midnight on the morning of January 14, 1860, disaster struck Seminary Hall. A fire broke out in a fireplace flue on the fifth floor. A group of girls fled toward the main part of town for help, while the women, under guidance of Ms. Peabody and other teachers, formed a bucket brigade, until Ms. Peabody declared it was impossible to stop

Originally built in 1855, the Western Seminary building was destroyed by fire in 1860 and 1871. This drawing shows the building in 1875. It would be renamed Peabody Hall in 1905. *Combination Atlas Map of Butler County, Ohio, L.H. Everts (1875), Lane Public Library Collection.*

the fire. She then informed the residents to gather what belongings they could and leave the building. All 175 women made it out of the building, thanks to the actions of Ms. Peabody. In a strange coincidence, the January 17, 1860, *Cincinnati Daily Commercial* mentions that on the previous day, Ms. Peabody had been discussing a deadly mill fire that occurred five nights earlier in Massachusetts that resulted in over two hundred dead. Ms. Peabody prophetically had said, "If the College should take fire, or any other accident occur, they [the students] might act in a thoughtful and collected manner." The fire completely destroyed the building, with many of the walls collapsing on themselves. The school resolved to rebuild quickly, and that they did.

When the plans were created for the new Seminary Hall, which opened in 1861, it was designed so the walls would not collapse in the unlikely event of another fire. That's exactly what happened on April 12, 1871: the new building erupted into flames, but the wall design worked as planned. All the walls remained standing after the fire. This time, the fire started near some wood stored for use in the bakery. Again, miraculously, all the students, staff and faculty survived. The walls were deemed structurally sound after the blaze, and the building was reconstructed and still stands today.

One strange event under Helen Peabody's tenure happened at around eleven o'clock in the evening on February 29, 1868, Leap Day. For weeks leading up to that night, the women in the seminary had believed someone had been entering the building at night and going through various rooms, desks and bags, looking for something. Nothing was known to have actually been stolen, just searched through; whatever the infiltrator was looking for, they weren't finding.

Two teachers decided to go into the first-floor library and wait to see if this trespasser might decide to show up again. When they heard footsteps ascending the basement stairs, then the stairs to the upper floors, they went to Ms. Peabody's room to tell her what had transpired. One teacher went to fetch the superintendent, Mr. Lyons. Mr. Lyons brought along his pistol and a friend, Mr. Henry Butler. The two men, three teachers and Ms. Peabody devised a plan to capture the burglar. The lower floor lights were all turned on, and Ms. Peabody watched the first floor. The two men went up the central staircase to the third floor, and three faculty members went up to the third floor by way of the stairways in the wings. This way, the intruder would be surrounded on the third floor.

The two men encountered the intruder, and after he ran into Butler, he yelled "Where am I?" and fled down the hall toward Lyons, who yelled at him to stop or he would shoot. The man did not stop, and Lyons, a man of his word, fired. The man then leapt over the banister and ran to the first floor. He failed to get the door open, then ran through a parlor, where Lyons caught up with him. The man threatened him by throwing furniture and saying he would kill him. The man then fled to the basement, back to the door where he had made his entry. Lyons fired three more shots, one at the top of the stairs and two while the man was unbolting the door, all the while yelling for the man to halt. Lyons and one of the teachers went out the basement door but didn't see the man. They decided to get more help. By then, other faculty and teachers had gathered, and a group went out and found the body of a large man, dead from multiple bullet wounds. They never found out what the man was looking for, and newspapers reported the strange fact that the man had magic charms sewn into his clothing, which they noted were proven to be ineffectual.

Peabody remained the principal of the school until June 17, 1887, when she resigned. She asked to be released, on the basis of her age (sixty-one), from the duties of her position for the rest of the year. It was said she was being exceedingly strict and had even expelled some students for things that were said to not warrant expulsion. She remained head of the school in name, and teachers actually ran it. In 1888, Leila McKee, an 1877 graduate, was made the second principal of the school. The school was renamed the Western: A College and Seminary for Women, and in 1904, the school changed its name again and became the Western College for Women. Finally, due to financial strain on the college, it was absorbed into Miami University in 1974. It is now known as the Western Campus of Miami University—confusingly for many who don't know the history, because it lies east of campus. In 1979, the Western Seminary Historic District was designated a U.S. Historic District.

The reason for Helen Peabody's request to vacate her position was said by some to be that she was not in favor of the school wanting to move away from religious teaching. Personally, she also had expressed interest in doing more missionary work. She traveled the world and lived in Pasadena, California, with her brother and his family until she passed away in 1905. After her passing, the school honored her by renaming Seminary Hall to Peabody Hall.

It's not known when students began telling stories about Helen Peabody haunting the hallowed halls of her namesake building. The basis of the

Peabody Hall as it stands today. *Author's collection.*

legend makes it sound like it occurred after the merger with Miami. The Western College graduated its last all-female class in June 1973. The buildings were refreshed and reopened as the Western Campus of Miami in 1974. It was now coed, something it was said Ms. Peabody did not agree with. She believed this because of her religious upbringing, how she was taught in school and how she led her school. It's said she especially likes to haunt men in her building.

Any definitive stories are hard to come by. There are the typical vague, generalized happenings such as people seeing her ghost or feeling a presence; others have claimed to hear screams coming from their phones, according to an October 30, 2015 *Miami Student* article. That article also makes mention of a ghost of a girl that committed suicide in the attic. Another article from the October 30, 1976 *Hamilton Journal-News* mentions a girl who hanged herself in her room; students who later lived in that room claimed to see the ghost of the hanging girl. It is not known if the two stories are versions of the same ghost or two different ghosts. Current research doesn't show anything to correlate with this, but suicides are not always reported in newspapers. The *Miami Student* reporter also talked to one student who was sitting alone in the lounge studying when the piano started playing by itself. The *Hamilton Journal-News* article has an organ story. In the 1930s, a girl frequently practiced the organ in the chapel. One morning, she was heard playing uncontrollably and at a fast pace. She had also gone insane. It was found out that she heard footsteps behind her but saw no one; the footsteps only stopped when she played. So play she did.

Peabody Hall folklore says the best way to bring about the ghost of Helen Peabody is to bring negative attention to yourself. Another superstition along the same lines seems to have been built around the portrait of Helen Peabody that hangs on the first floor. You are to be on your best behavior and not say anything improper around her portrait. According to an anonymous Reddit post in 2011, a couple roommates did just that. They talked unflatteringly about Ms. Peabody to her portrait and felt her wrath a short time later. The night began while they were studying for exams and a large stack of books fell over. While they were stacking them back up, a lamp fell to the floor. They set everything back how it was and resumed studying, until the lamp fell over again. While setting the lamp up the second time, they noticed a flashing light on the phone; somehow, they'd gotten a message, even though the phone never rang. They checked, and there were no new messages to be played. Again, they returned to studying, until the lamp fell for a third time and the message light flashed again. Yet again, no messages. So this time they unplugged the phone and put it in the middle of the room. As they once again got back into study mode, something began beating from inside the closet! Then they noticed the unplugged phone had a glowing message light again.

The students were undoubtedly shaken by the events. They left their room with the phone and went to speak to their resident advisor. They explained to the RA what had been happening and the RA said he would talk to the office of telecommunications to see if there were issues with their phone lines.

By this time, the two men were exhausted. They had bunk beds in the dorm, and the bigger student, who happened to be a linebacker on the football team, was on the bottom bunk. He was also a notoriously light sleeper. In the middle of the night, the beating in the closet happened again. The roommate on the upper bunk jumped down and turned on the light, but his light-sleeping roommate wasn't budging. The roommate tried to wake the other man up, which usually was a pretty easy task, but not this time. As he finally gave up and turned to leave the room to get help, the other man got up and mumbled something incoherent, then lay back down. Knowing his roommate was alive and deciding they were both just extremely exhausted from the strange events earlier that evening, he was determined to go to sleep and found a vacant room so he was not awakened again by the beating of the closet door.

The next morning, when he got back to his room, he asked his roommate why he didn't wake up and if he remembered his friend yelling at him, trying to wake him. His friend replied that he remembered a woman in his dream standing over him, holding him down and yelling at him. He couldn't describe her, but they both thought it was Ms. Peabody.

Later, the RA came to their room with a new phone. The office of telecommunications said they had two hundred missed calls and one message. When they played the message back, it was the insulting chat they had in front of Helen Peabody's portrait, in hopes of stirring up the ghost. Whether or not this is a factual account of the ghost of Ms. Peabody or a cautionary tale, it gets the point across to not anger Helen Peabody in her building.

Another story about Helen Peabody comes by way of the Miami school website in a promotional piece for a 2018 play that was written and performed by Miami students and alumni called *Echoes of Miami*. It was a play telling the tales of the ghosts and legends of the school. The play featured three actresses in the role of Helen Peabody. One of the actresses told the reporter about a time she saw a large prop fall from a shelf with no explanation. She said it was pretty common to have those types of occurrences behind the scenes. One of the production team members was a medium and would give the cast updates on things that happened. Odd things would happen so often that the cast and crew just began speaking to Ms. Peabody to acknowledge her. So it seems that maybe Ms. Peabody isn't just confined to the Western Female College.

The *Miami Student* article from 2015 also mentions that the spirit has been seen under the stone Western bridges. This does correlate to another urban legend that Ms. Peabody walks from her grave plot to Peabody Hall, as they are relatively close to each other. Her ashes were returned to Oxford from California and interred in the Oxford Cemetery in 1906, with a procession of three hundred students from the Western College for Women to the cemetery. Ms. Peabody was a strong woman, in her deeds, running a school and in her faith. She gained respect in life and seeks to keep it in death.

THE RED HANDS OF REID HALL

The reported hauntings in Reid Hall at Miami University were popular ghost stories told around campus while the building stood and even after its demolition in 2007. The reason is that they were based on an infamous tragic event on campus: a love triangle gone wrong and an innocent man trying to bring calm to the situation.

> *MIAMI STUDENT DEAD IN REID HALL GUNPLAY;*
> *FRESHMAN SUSPECT CRITICAL OF SELF WOUND*
> *Counselor Fatally Shot, Third Wounded in Fray;*
> *Cite Argument Over Girl*
> —Hamilton Journal and Daily News, *Saturday, May 9, 1959*

The previous night, freshman James Walker was walking his date, freshman Sandra Epps, back to Wells Hall after seeing a movie. As they made their way to Sandra's dorm around eleven thirty, they were approached by fellow freshman Henry A. Lucas. Lucas had also been dating Ms. Epps. Some words were said between the men; Sandra said they just talked, the young men didn't argue and it wasn't a heated exchange.

Whatever was said did not sit well with Lucas. After he confronted the couple, he went to Fisher Hall, where he broke into the building. Fisher

Hall was where the Navy ROTC firing range was located. Lucas had been a member of the Navy ROTC until recently, when he was dismissed due to poor grades. He broke into the gun cabinet and stole two .22-caliber handguns and about three hundred rounds of ammunition, according to news reports.

On leaving Fisher Hall, Lucas went to Reid Hall at around one o'clock in the morning and went to the second floor, room 226, where James Walker lived. When Walker opened the door, he was greeted by an angry Lucas, who challenged him to a fight. An argument broke out between the two, until Walker told Lucas to leave him alone and said he was going back to bed. When he turned around, Lucas pulled out a pistol and shot at Walker, grazing his neck.

On hearing the commotion, Roger Sayles, a dormitory councilor, came out to check on matters. What exactly happened next isn't quite clear, but it seems Sayles tried to stop Lucas from fleeing the building and was shot in the process. He was shot in the temple, probably dying instantly; some reports say he was shot in the chest also. There were reportedly three shots fired, because police recovered three spent cartridges. Sayles's body was found slumped against a wall, around the corner and down a corridor from Walker's room.

Lucas fled the building and made his way to the second floor of Ogden Hall, where there was a phone booth. He called Sandra Epps around 1:55 a.m., and she told him that at least one of the people he had shot was dead.

It was a terrifying scene on campus the following morning; the manhunt had gone on all night. The manhunt was on for Lucas; search parties included Miami University Police, Oxford Police, state patrolmen, deputy sheriffs and twelve men from the sheriff's mounted division. Roads were blocked going in and out of town; the heaviest part of the search was in the woods near Oxford. Finally, Lucas was found at 7:55 a.m. by a student in Ogden Hall at the bottom of the phone booth. After the phone call to Ms. Epps, Lucas had written a note and shot himself in the head, but he was still alive. In the note, Lucas admitted to shooting the two men; the coroner also said the note showed "signs of mental strain." Lucas succumbed to the self-inflicted wound later that day. It was also found out that Lucas had visited the hospital just a few nights prior. On that Thursday night, he was admitted to the hospital at 9:28. Earlier that evening, he had gone to a professor's home to discuss a paper he was writing. He became ill and an ambulance was called; no other details were given. It was another sad addendum to the story.

After the night of horror in Reid Hall, many students began hearing things, mainly footsteps from unknown and unseen visitors and doors that would open and close on their own. Those were the things that couldn't be seen, but there was something that could be seen and wouldn't go away. According to school legend, when Roger Sayles was shot, he fell against a door in the hallway and left two bloody handprints on the door. The handprints supposedly remained for decades. As for the sounds of ghostly footsteps and doors opening and closing of their own accord, they were always attributed to the ghost of Sayles, still roaming Reid Hall where he was killed. It sounds like a residual haunting, which is a traumatic event repeating itself over and over, and in this case the spirit could be Sayles or Lucas.

The Phantom of Oxford

It is probably the most well-known missing persons case in all of Ohio, if not the Midwest. It's a puzzling mystery that baffles everyone who has studied it. It's been the focus of many articles, documentaries and podcasts, and there is even a website dedicated to finding the truth seventy years later. The victim has the haunting sobriquet "the Phantom of Oxford," which was also the title of a 1976 documentary. The year he disappeared, nineteen-year-old Ronald Tammen was a Miami University sophomore and a resident advisor in his dormitory. He was known around campus as a wrestler, bass player and Delta Tau Delta fraternity member. His story ends on April 19, 1953, in Fisher Hall.

Fisher Hall began as the Oxford Female College and was founded by Reverend Dr. John Witherspoon Scott, the son-in-law of President Benjamin Harrison. Constructed over a period of four years, the building was dedicated on September 3, 1856. It had a large central tower surrounded by wide wings. In 1867, the Oxford Female College merged with the Oxford Female Institute, and the building was used as a dormitory. Dr. George F. Cook purchased the building, and it was transformed from a college building into the sanitarium known as the Oxford Retreat in 1882. The retreat stood on a spacious forty-acre area with woods, a stream and walking paths. It afforded the best care to its patients, who were there for reasons of mental and nervous afflictions, including drug and alcohol addiction.

Sadly, escapes and suicide attempts were not uncommon in institutions like this. There were multiple newspaper reports over the years of people

An undated photo of Fisher Hall, where Ronald Tammen disappeared on April 19, 1953. *Miami University Archives, Frank R. Snyder Collection.*

who had escaped and were usually found in Hamilton or Cincinnati train depots and returned. There were also many reports of patients hanging themselves, using cloth cords and ropes fashioned from twine. Most bizarrely, one woman, Alice Brown, used her own hair to hang herself in her closet. Other methods were jumping from windows and drinking acid. One man who was a trusty, a status that gave him more freedom than a regular inmate, whom no one felt was a threat to others or himself, was found with his throat slit ear to ear. On July 21, 1898, a *Butler County Democrat* article mentioned a Mrs. Sterns who had hanged herself at the retreat; it was kept secret until a township employee notified the county coroner, who was rather displeased and planned to question Dr. Cook about the matter. It makes one wonder how many suicides may not have been reported.

In 1925, the building known as the Oxford Retreat was sold by Dr. Cook to Miami University. Dr. R. Harvey Cook retained the annex building known as the Pines, which eventually became Wilson Hall. Miami University remodeled the building, removed the bars from the windows to suit the requirements to serve as a men's dormitory and renamed it Fisher Hall after a former trustee, Judge Elam Fisher. Legend has it that when he was a student at Miami, he was expelled while courting a woman at the Oxford Female College due to some infraction at the very building that later was named for him. It served as a men's dormitory until 1941, then it became a naval training school during World War II. In 1944–45, it served as a women's dorm, returned to being a men's hall until 1958, then housed female students until 1961. At that point, the upper floors were in a state of disrepair, and the first floor was occupied by the theater department until 1968. After that, the onetime jewel of the Oxford Female College and storied sanitarium became a giant storage center. It was entered in the National Register of Historic Places in 1978, then by the end of the year, it had been removed from the list, because the university deemed it would be better to tear down a historic building than renovate it, even though the cost estimates were roughly the same. As the building came down, searches were conducted for the remains of Ronald Tammen in the rubble, including in wells and cisterns under the building. Nothing was found.

The lingering question remains: What happened to Ron Tammen? Born Ronald Henry Tammen Jr. on July 23, 1933, in the Cleveland suburb of Maple Heights, Ohio, Ron Tammen was the middle child of five siblings. He was described as a handsome man and had two distinguishing features, a cauliflower ear from wrestling and a crooked tooth. He always seemed busy, usually studying in his room, at the fraternity house or playing in his band, the Campus Owls.

On the blustery, snow flurry–filled evening of Sunday, April 19, 1953, around seven o'clock, Tammen was a few doors down from his room helping a friend, Richard Titus, with some homework. Sometime before eight o'clock, Tammen went back to his room and discovered a dead fish in his bed. It apparently had been placed there earlier by his friend Titus as a prank. Oddly, Titus didn't admit that to anyone for nearly six decades, when he told Jennifer Wenger, the creator of the website A Good Man Is Hard to Find (www.ronaldtammen.com/). It was around eight o'clock when Tammen went to get a clean set of sheets. The residence hall manager remarked that he looked very tired. He replied that he planned to go to bed as soon as he put the new sheets on. His roommate, Chuck Findley, arrived back at the dorm around ten thirty after a weekend in Dayton. He entered the room expecting to see Tammen. The lights were on, Tammen's book was open on his desk and there was music playing. He assumed Tammen must have gone to his fraternity house, and when he didn't come back to the dorm, Findley assumed he must have slept there.

On Monday, after not seeing Tammen, Findley made a check at the fraternity house, and the fraternity members said he had not been there. School officials were notified and began trying to find information about where Tammen went. When they examined his room, it was found that he had left his keys and his wallet, with no cash but his driver's license and draft card. His fraternity pin was placed on top of his keys, and his class ring was also left behind. The only thing of note missing was his watch. His car was in the parking lot, with his bass fiddle in the backseat. He simply blinked from existence.

Many other theories, anomalies and possible bits of evidence revealed themselves during the ensuing decades. Some said the fish in the bed wasn't left by Titus; it was a message that Ron was going to "sleep with the fishes," in mafioso speak. There was a report that Tammen was seen leaving in a car driven by a "woman from Hamilton." Others believe that Tammen was secretly recruited by the CIA. Some strange bits of evidence have been found by intrepid researchers like Joe Cella of the *Hamilton Journal News* and Jennifer Wenger of A Good Man Is Hard to Find.

Many believe Tammen's ghost haunted Fisher Hall before it was torn down. Others have claimed it was haunted years before his disappearance. One legend supposedly took place when it was the Oxford Female College dormitory. A group of girls was socializing in a downstairs room when one said she was going to retire early. Hours later, her roommate went upstairs to go to bed, and she found her roommate's bed empty. In the middle of the night, she heard a scratching at the door. She did not get up to answer it; she ignored it and fell back to sleep. The next morning, she opened the door to find her roommate dead in the hall, murdered with a hatchet. It's not clear when that story began being told; it has the telltale signs of an urban legend. It is strange that it involves a missing roommate in that building; it may have been inspired by Tammen's disappearance.

Students have claimed to hear strange noises and doors slamming and see shadowy figures and statues that moved. One professor reported that people outside saw a light on the third floor. There were no lights or even power supplied to that floor at that time, and the door to the third floor was always locked. The auditorium lights would dim for no reason. The bust of Elam Fisher that was in the building inexplicably disappeared only to appear in other locations, even appearing on the locked third floor once. There were even claims that an apparition of Elam Fisher was seen in the building. Some also claimed to have seen the spirit of Tammen.

Shortly after Tammen's disappearance, stories began of voices and singing being heard outside of Fisher Hall in the formal garden. Students went to investigate and saw a white figure run through the area. It sounds likely that this was a college prank, except the figure was said to have moved at superhuman speed. Other students and even professors began to admit they had been subject to some unexplainable events, from slamming doors to being followed by footsteps, with the footsteps even following them from floor to floor.

The hauntings actually became so frequent when the theater department moved to Fisher Hall that the department hired a psychic medium to hold a séance. In October 1967, the theater department began looking for a medium who could find the answer to who had been haunting the students in the building. They had originally planned to do it as part of their annual Halloween party but found all the psychics in the area were booked up due to the Halloween season. A self-proclaimed retired spiritualist minister, John Lilley of Dayton, agreed to conduct the séance on November 18, 1967, under the auspices of a full moon. The goal was to determine the identity of the ghost. The students believed the ghost was Judge Elam Fisher, Fisher Hall's namesake. Some believed the ghost to be Ron Tammen. Oddly, no one ever mentioned that the ghosts might be from the days of the Oxford Retreat, which seems the most logical choice, given its past. Prior to the séance, Lilley confirmed the building was definitely haunted, because as he did a walkthrough, he conversed with three entities.

The event, limited to two hundred tickets, was sold out, with an overflow crowd wanting to get in. However, the *Middletown Journal* and *Hamilton Daily News Journal* reported that the séance was a disaster. Lilley began well, discussing religious spiritualism and types and classes of mediums, then he went into a trance and delivered an hour-long sermon. His voice and appearance didn't change; he just said he was the spirit of Harrison Barret, a medium from the late 1800s, and began preaching. He spoke nothing of the ghosts of Fisher Hall. When he asked for questions, someone asked if he felt anything violent had happened in the building. Barret said he would have to defer that question to another spirit and "left" Lilley.

The second spirit to "enter" Lilley affected a change in his voice—sadly, a stereotypical Native American voice that began by saying, "Me am Indian chief when lived on earth…" This spirit claimed to be Chief Falling Waters, occasionally Running Waters. He went on to say that there was foul play on the land 150 years prior, and a missing man was not found. He also said that forty years ago, a man was strangled near Fisher Hall by three men and his body was taken to a medical school near Columbus. Chief Falling/Running Waters then went on to claim that Ron Tammen had his throat slit in the back of the building by three students and one outsider. They stripped the body and dumped him in the Ohio River.

The audience became increasingly irate throughout, and many walked out; others laughed like it was a comedy show, pointing out the errors in the stories. Some questioned the fact that the two-hundred-year-old chief was using present-day vernacular sometimes and spoke like a racist cartoon at other times.

Lilley had brought along two other mediums, one a woman known only as Mrs. Ross who did her best to save the séance when Lilley said he was exhausted from channeling the spirits. Mrs. Ross was able to show off a more believable display of clairvoyant powers with the remaining audience. She answered personal questions posed by the audience members, some vague but many strangely precise, which brought the heckling and tensions down. She also cautioned people not to laugh at what they didn't know. She then claimed that specific questions about the building couldn't be answered, because the answers could lead to someone being hurt. Following that, she saw a vision—a vision of a knife with the initials J.S. and blood, on the handle. That was all that was mentioned.

Lilley, recovered from his exhaustion or embarrassment, returned to tell his life story and how he became a medium, and the news reports said that he came off as sincere in his beliefs, but it was doubtful that anyone else in the hall believed him that night.

Even though the séance was a bust, the stories of the hauntings of Fisher Hall grew in popularity. It became a local legend, with Miami and high school students venturing to the building, hoping to interact with the spirits. There were occasional reports of arrests for breaking and entering. The building was still being used for storage, and a guard was assigned to night watch duty, saying the only sounds he heard were people breaking the wood covering the windows to get in.

A guard wasn't on duty in the spring of 1972 when six Talawanda High School girls did what you're never supposed to do at a haunted place. A May 10, 1972, *Cincinnati Post* article tells a story that begins like a classic horror movie. During a weekend slumber party, the girls decided it might be fun to recite incantations out of a witchcraft book in front of Fisher Hall. They approached the forlorn and off-limits building, proceeded to sit in a circle on the lawn and lit a candle. One girl placed the book in front of her so she could read the bewitching text, and they all joined hands. They proclaimed, "We summon you!" and the candle flame got larger and brighter. Then they all had a wave of foreboding wash over them. They felt that whatever they'd summoned did not want them interfering with it. It seemed like a presence that had been locked in the building for ages. One girl looked up and noticed a large group of what she thought was fireflies and a black "shape" slowly moving down the building. One girl said that they were getting fearful of something that was not physical but spiritual. They all spontaneously broke their circle to leave, and when they did, their sense of fear became stronger. One of the girls remembered that the book said they must send the spirit away before breaking the circle of incantation. They hastily lit the candle and rejoined hands, dismissing the spirit. The sense of fear immediately seemed to subside.

The Miami University Planning Commission conducted walking tours in 1973 to show people the state the building was in and discuss ways to rehabilitate it. They conducted two tours, because the first one was very popular. A man who was on the first tour documented it with an audio recorder. He came back for the second tour to ask if there was a radio or anyone playing a flute during the previous tour. The guide said there was no one else in the building and no radios or record players. The man had used a brand-new tape, and he had clearly caught flute music on his recordings.

The long history of the building known as Fisher Hall came to an end in 1978. It was replaced by the Marcum Center, opened in 1981, now just called the Marcum after its 2012 renovation. The building offers a hotel and conference center on campus. There are still formal gardens but no reports of a singing entity in white that moves at superhuman speed or any other ghost stories.

The Spirits of the Sanitarium

Wilson Hall has a long and storied history. It actually was only known as Wilson Hall for the last thirty-three years of its existence. It began as a secondary annex for the Oxford Retreat. The original building that was built on the spot was a wood structure called the Pines. It was made from local pine and was also surrounded by pines, which is how it received its name. It was thought to have been built in the 1840s and was originally known as the Lane and McGregor homestead. It was known as a place where the most ostentatious residents of early Oxford would gather socially.

Before the Oxford Retreat's main building was sold to Miami University, all the patients were relocated to the main building while renovations were being completed on the Pines. The night of June 12, 1925, as Dr. and Mrs. Cook returned to the main building, they smelled pine smoke in the air. The night watchman approached them and said he had been smelling it for about fifteen minutes and couldn't locate the source. About that same time, the Cooks' son, Dr. Malcomb Cook, was returning home and also noticed the smell. He walked down to check on the Pines. When he was about halfway there, he saw flames at the back of the structure. He yelled for his parents and the watchman. Dr. Harvey Cook ran in and tried to use the firehose in the building, but the flames were spreading too fast. He suffered some burns trying to save the building. The *Hamilton Evening Journal* said the fire might have been the most spectacular ever seen in Oxford as the stately pines burst into flame around the burning building. By morning, all that was left was a single chimney.

Miami agreed to allow the patients to stay in the main building until the Pines was rebuilt. The new two-story structure used native blue limestone and was topped with a red tile roof. It had a large front porch with a two-story roof supported by four large columns. Dr. Cook also had a home, Cook Place, built nearby. The patients were transferred to the new building in May 1926.

In 1936, Miami University purchased the buildings and the fourteen-acre site, with the stipulation that the Cooks could stay in their home for life. The Pines was converted into a women's dormitory. It changed between male and female dormitories over the years until 1972, when it became co-ed. It also housed the radio operator trainees who were in the U.S. Navy

Wilson Hall, a.k.a. the Pines, circa 1986. *Miami University Archives, Frank R. Snyder Collection.*

training school from 1942 until 1946. The year 1986 brought a new name to the building; no longer the Pines, it became Wilson Hall, named after Dr. Charles Wilson, a Miami alumnus. In 2010, during a survey of the dormitories on campus, the building—built of stone and concrete to survive fires after its predecessor burned—was now deemed a high risk of being a fire hazard. In 2019, it was decided that the building was too expensive to bring up to modern standards, and it was demolished. Cook Place does remain and was remodeled after the Cooks' deaths. Mrs. Cook passed away in 1948, followed by Dr. Cook a year later. In 1951, it became the home for the provosts, and in 1970, it became an administrative office.

Being a former sanitarium, there were a few stories. Many people have said the building did have a creepy feeling. People attributed anything out of the ordinary to hauntings by former patients. One very strange legend says that if you leave your shoes out in the hallway, the next morning, they will be polished. This seems like maybe it would have been tied to the building being a former U.S. Navy barracks, but oddly enough, people said it was Dr. Cook doing the polishing. There are tales of doors opening and closing and basement lights flickering, typically only during the day. Students said there were still cell-like structures in the third-floor attic, with the names of former patients written on the wall or on paper tags affixed to the floor. Actually, these were storage areas from when the building was a dormitory. The basement allegedly had a bathtub that was used for shock therapy. There was also supposedly a tunnel connecting Dr. Cook's house to the building's basement. It was said to have been built because the women that received shock treatment would panic when they saw him from the window as he was walking to the Pines to administer yet another treatment. Bathtubs were also used for cold-water immersion, which were probably done at the Pines, but electroshock therapy was developed in 1938, two years after Miami University purchased the building. Now that the building is gone, where could the spirits go?

A student at Miami, Frank Munafo, told me that one of his roommates was on a different schedule than everyone else and would usually go to bed very late at night or early in the morning, while the other two roommates were sleeping. One early morning, when he walked into the room, he looked over at Frank's bed and saw the black shape of a man standing and staring over Frank while he was sleeping, then he vanished. This happened at least three times. Another morning, Frank woke up with a flower on his pillow next to him. The roommates swore they didn't leave it. It makes one wonder if Dr. Cook is still doing rounds. There is no longer a Wilson Hall, but there is a nearby McBride Hall that is full of students to keep watch over.

CHAPTER 8
TOMBSTONE TALES

ROSSVILLE REVENANTS

When Rossville was laid out, a fractional lot along Boudinout Street, now Park Avenue, was set aside as the Rossville Burying Ground. It is now known as Sutherland Park, named for John Sutherland, one of the men who donated parcels for creation of the cemetery. A plaque on a rock at the southeast corner of the park at Park Avenue and North D Street reads:

Sutherland Park
Pioneer Burial Ground—1804

Stranger, pause as you pass by
As you are now, so once was I
As I am now, so you must be
Prepare for death and follow me

And God shall wipe away all tears

The plaque further explains that these were popular epitaphs carved on many of the stones and "due to deterioration of the cemetery, many bodies were removed in 1848 to the new Greenwood Cemetery." It doesn't say "all."

Legal burials were supposed to have ended with the removal of the bodies. In some cases, the bodies may have been moved but not the tombstones.

An 1840s artist's depiction near the Rossville Burying Ground looking east across the river toward Hamilton. The courthouse and covered bridge can be seen in the background. *Lane Public Library, George C. Cummins "Remember When" Photograph Collection.*

An 1888 *Hamilton Democrat* article reported that burials took place at least until 1863. In 1878, plans called for covering up the remaining tombstones and stipulated that "each base head and footstone must be buried on its respective grave with the lettered side of the stone up so that the top of the stone will be 18 inches below the surface of the ground." The workers did not take great care in converting the former burial site into a city park. The *Hamilton Democrat* stated:

> Some of the graves are not marked and other tablets had been destroyed. Since the contractor and force have gone to work, no attention has been paid to the last resting place of the pioneers of Butler County. The marks of respect have been roughly broken, thrown in a pile, and the relative could not pick out the stones and inscriptions from the chaos. Worse than that, the graves are scooped open, coffins broken, and the skeletons exposed to view. Yesterday children were playing with the bones of pioneers.

Nearby residents began to notice dark shapes moving among the tombstones of the disturbed cemetery at night. People continued to see those shadows at night for decades.

One of the biggest scourges to hit the world in the nineteenth century was cholera, which arrived in Butler County in 1832. In Stella Weiler Taylor's December 5, 1931, *Hamilton Evening Journal* column titled Rosemary, That's for Remembrance, she describes the tombstones in the cemetery as she remembers them in her youth and tells a ghost story.

> *I saw the leaning "mossy marbles," tottering like aged men,*
> *above the places where the rude forefathers of the hamlet slept.*

She related a tale from resident Walter Lee: in 1833, during the cholera pandemic, a beautiful young girl came down with the horrible sickness and died only a few days before her wedding day. Before she died, she said that she wished to be buried in her beautiful bride dress—and she was. Soon after her burial, her heartbroken betrothed was found slumped over the flower-covered grave. He was not in mourning any longer; he was dead from a self-inflicted bullet wound through his heart. The man was buried next to his love. According to the legend, at midnight on what would have been their wedding day, the ghostly spirits rise from their graves and stroll hand in hand through the cemetery. Mr. Lee went on to say that he and his friends never saw them because they didn't know the exact date to look. He shared a poem that was based on the legend:

> *Again the lovers' tryst is kept*
> *Where our forefathers long have slept*
> *At midnight's weird and solemn hours*
> *Amid the trees and blooming flowers*
> *And as in life, the same in death,*
> *When springtime gives its fragrant breath*
> *They stroll amid the silent tombs*
> *And pluck again the rose's blooms.*

From the poem, we can deduce that the apparitions appear in the spring, when the flowers are blooming and fragrant. Any further clues, such as names, are lost to history. Local cemetery records do not show any burials fitting the criteria. Are the lovers still buried under the soil of the park?

Every few decades, the headstones make a reappearance. In October 1964, a city crew installing a new gas line across the park uncovered tombstones. Thirty years later, in 1994, headstones were again unintentionally uncovered. It's not known how many headstones, or bodies, may remain in the park.

According to some members of the Hamilton Ghost Stories Facebook group, people who live near Sutherland Park have reported strange things in their homes. People have reported hearing footsteps and anomalous photos. One resident told a story about her granddaughter's experience. As she slept in her room, the little girl felt cold air and what she described as sparkling lights, followed by a woman in a blue dress walking by her door, who turned to look at her—and had no eyes. Up until the 1850s, wedding dresses were most commonly white, gold or blue. Another grandmother told of her granddaughter who had an invisible friend. The invisible friend said she was eighteen and named Abby. Could these be the same spirit or the bride?

The Ghosts of Greenwood

As Hamilton and Rossville continued to grow in the mid-nineteenth century, the communities wanted to create a single large cemetery on the outskirts of Hamilton for use by both towns. The Rossville Burying Ground and the Hamilton Burial Ground originally were on the outskirts of town, but by the mid-1800s, neighborhoods had developed around them. Another burgeoning worldwide cholera epidemic was also making its way across Asia and Europe, and everyone knew it was only a matter of time before it reached the United States. The area had suffered greatly from the previous outbreak in the early 1830s. Greenwood Cemetery Association was established in 1848. Land was purchased from David Bingham, and the dearly departed from the Rossville and Hamilton Burial Grounds were removed to the new Greenlawn Cemetery.

Greenlawn Cemetery was planned by renowned landscape architect Adolph Strauch. Greenwood's design was inspired by Spring Grove Cemetery and Boston's Mt. Auburn Cemetery, both designed by Strauch. Greenwood is in the style of a park with winding paths, landscaping and art in the form of monuments and statuary. In 1994, the older original section of Greenwood Cemetery, the area south of Greenwood Avenue, was placed on the U.S. National Register of Historic Places.

When traversing the cemetery grounds, the most striking structure you will see is the public receiving vault, built in 1892 in the Romanesque Revival style. The stone structure was constructed into a hillside in the northwest corner of the cemetery, facing what used to be the lake, which now has been filled for the expansion of lots. In the days when graves

Greenwood Cemetery circa 1870s. From L.H. Everts's *1875 Combination Atlas Map of Butler County, Ohio. Lane Public Library Collection.*

were only dug by hand, the frozen ground could be impenetrable during the winter months. Receiving vaults were built to store the coffins holding the deceased until the ground was able to be hand dug. There was an underground vault that was in use before the 1892 public receiving vault was built. It was basically an eight-by-twelve-foot hole in the ground that would have held six to eight caskets.

This story comes from Rick Fornshell and happened when he was very young and lived near Greenwood Cemetery. The cemetery was a wondrous place for kids to play ditch, hide-and-seek and other games among the large trees and tombstones. One night, the kids were in the cemetery after dark playing a game of hide-and-seek. Rick headed toward the lake in the rear of the cemetery. The lake no longer exists but has been drained and filled gradually over time with the expansions of the veterans' burial areas. It originally covered a large area at the back of the cemetery. When Rick was playing hide-and-seek with his friends, he found a low spot near a crypt on the hillside near this area. It was a spot he had used many other times, and it was a great place to hide. That night, as he peeked over the stone of the crypt, he noticed something very unusual. When he looked toward the public receiving vault door, he saw a misty shape in front of the door. The mist had an eerie faint glow and proceeded to go through the door and into the building. At that point, winning the game of hide-and-seek was the last thing on his mind, and he ran home.

The Greenwood Cemetery public receiving vault was built in 1892 to house bodies in winter months when graves could not be hand dug. *Author's collection.*

On Friday, June 11, 1932, Eugene Blattau and Alfred Garrod, both age eight, went from Eugene's home on Noble Avenue in Lindenwald to the Great Miami River to catch tadpoles. According to the June 11 *Hamilton Evening Journal*, Eugene fell ten feet into eight feet of water "at the foot of Forest Avenue." This would be roughly where North Riverview Drive and River Road are currently located. The river used to flow along where River Road is now, and there was a large island in the river at that location. That area has been reshaped and portions filled in to redirect the river over the years.

In his pursuit of tadpoles, Eugene tried to climb down the embankment and slipped, falling into the water below. He was unable to swim. Alfred, standing helpless atop the embankment, saw Eugene sink below the water. He quickly ran to the nearest house, screaming that Gene had drowned. Some men ran to help and pulled the boy's lifeless body out of the river. The Hamilton fire department arrived and tried to resuscitate the boy to no avail. The young man was buried in Greenwood Cemetery the following Monday.

This story came from the Hamilton Ghost Stories Facebook group. One late August evening in the late '60s or early '70s, a group of children had finished playing hide-and-seek in Greenwood Cemetery. They knew the story of Eugene Blattau's ghost being seen at the cemetery, as it was a popular neighborhood legend. They decided to check it out as they were on their way out of the cemetery. As they walked near his grave site, they crested a hill and saw what looked like a young boy standing by the grave, wearing a shimmering white shirt. Two of the boys tried to get closer, and the boy vanished, followed by a short, cold breeze that blew past them on the hot muggy night.

On November 20, 1943, as part of Operation Galvanic, a U.S. Marines division landed on Betio Island in the Gilbert Islands. Its goal was to recapture the island from the invading Japanese and ultimately take control of the Japanese airfield, in what would be known as the Battle of Tarawa. One of those valiant men who gave their lives that day in that important American victory in the Pacific was twenty-two-year-old Pharmacist's Mate Second Class Tommy Murphy of the Third Battalion of the Eighth Marines.

At the time of the invasion, this was the largest force yet assembled in the Pacific. During the heat of the battle, young Tommy was shot on the deck of his boat. As a pharmacist's mate second class, it's very probable that he was killed as he was delivering medical assistance to others. Just short of one thousand American men were killed or would lose their lives as the result of wounds obtained during the seventy-two-hour battle. When that many died in such a short time, and also during periods of heavy fighting, burials were swift and slipshod. Sadly, some graves became obscured or went unnoticed as burial areas. Most of the fallen were repatriated and buried in the United States; however, over one hundred were unaccounted for. Thomas Jesse Murphy was one of them. On March 5, 1944, the *Indianapolis Star* reported that his mother, in Greencastle, Indiana, received word that her son was killed in action during the Battle of Tarawa. Almost five years later, on February 7, 1949, Murphy's remains were deemed unrecoverable by the military.

According to a local North End neighborhood legend, with nobody to bury, the family had a cenotaph installed at Greenwood Cemetery. A cenotaph is a gravestone with no body. Its purpose is to serve as a memorial to the missing or those buried elsewhere. Although he was born and raised in Greencastle, Indiana, the memorial marker was placed in Greenwood Cemetery by his half-brother who lived in Hamilton.

The legend goes that after the stone was placed in the cemetery, neighbors along Greenwood Avenue began hearing a sound like a gunshot followed by a scream. What were these strange sounds? Some thought the screams had an easily explainable origin, such as an animal; others thought it was Tommy

Medics administer first aid to an injured soldier after the Battle of Tarawa in the Gilbert Islands, November 1943. *National Archives.*

screaming from his monument because he didn't want to be forgotten on some atoll in the Pacific.

Although Tommy Murphy's remains were deemed unrecoverable, there was hope. In late 2013, the remains of one American and four Japanese were uncovered on a preserved battle site. In March 2015, as a footer was being dug for a carport, a man noticed he had dug up the dog tag of an American soldier. An investigation was conducted, and the remains of thirty-six missing American soldiers were found and recovered. After the temporary battle cemetery was lost and retaken by nature, it was paved over as a parking lot. Four years later, in March 2019, another twenty-two bodies of missing marines were recovered.

The remains found in March 2015 made it back to American soil at Joint Base Pearl Harbor-Hickam in Honolulu, Hawaii. In October 2017, Tommy Murphy's remains were identified in that group. His remains were returned to the family just before Memorial Day in 2018. They arrived at the Cincinnati/Northern Kentucky Airport, followed by an escort from the

Patriot Guard back to Zettler Funeral Home in Hamilton. Services were that Sunday, and Tommy was finally laid to rest in American soil at eleven o'clock in the morning on Memorial Day 2018. After seventy-five years, Thomas Jesse Murphy was home.

THE SHADOWS OF THE COFFIN FACTORY

In his book *Madison Township Bicentennial Sketches (1799–1999)*, local historian George C. Crout mentions a haunted house that still stood, as of 1999, east of the Elk Creek Cemetery in Madison Township. In the 1830s, this house belonged to Thomas Wilson, and the coffins were built in the shed, with the funerals being conducted at Wilson's home by his partner, Charles Miller. Crout supports the stories by saying that poet, author and historian William Henry Venable recounted some of these stories about the schoolhouse that was next to the cemetery. Venable said that people told of "seeing spooks about the place" and that "ghosts were surrounded by lights and would rise in the air from the old coffin factory, flying to the old graveyard to the west."

The old entry gates to Elk Creek Cemetery. Ghostly shadows were said to be seen traveling between the cemetery and the nearby Wilson Coffin factory. *Author's collection.*

There is at least one house dating from 1837 that could fit the description. Thomas Wilson moved to Middletown in 1839. He was employed as a furniture maker and cabinetmaker; during that time, cabinetmakers also made coffins. As a matter of fact, Thomas Wilson, by 1880, decided to forego the furniture and cabinetry craft and focus solely on the undertaking business. His legacy continues today, with Middletown's Wilson-Schramm-Spaulding Funeral Home still providing the services Wilson did nearly two centuries ago. Thomas Wilson brought many innovations to Middletown, such as the first horse-drawn ornamental hearse in 1862.

The first burial in Madison Township's Elk Creek Cemetery was said to have been that of a six-year-old boy named Millener. His headstone, like many others used at that time in the cemetery, was made from local limestone. Over the years, his name was lost due to the erosion of the stone. In 1811, the United Brethren Church was organized, with John Kemp as the original minister. The cemetery still has a cornerstone from the 1848 church building located near the back of the cemetery.

Millville's Haunted Cemetery

Millville Cemetery, in Hanover Township, was founded in 1822. The town received the name Millville after the gristmill built by Joel Williams for Joseph Van Horn in 1805. The cemetery is located between the city of Hamilton and the village of Millville on State Route 129, named Millville Avenue in this location.

The cemetery has a few nameless spirits that still allegedly wander the grounds. A young girl has been seen toward the back of the cemetery looking out over the farm fields behind. A ghostly elderly gentleman has appeared wandering through the tombstones. Also, a glowing orb has been observed floating through the cemetery grounds.

Reily Cemetery's Spirits

The Reily Cemetery is located just southwest of the town on Peoria-Reily Road. It was founded in 1833 and still operates today. One feature you will easily notice is the Native American mound located in the rear of the

Gate to Reily Cemetery. *Author's collection.*

cemetery. The mound was excavated in the early 1800s, where it was found to have contained many clay vessels.

There are also multiple ghost stories. When a young girl was buried, her family placed a life-size metal statue of her favorite pet on her tombstone. Rumors began that the dog had been encased inside. Also, when you drive through the east gate and around the loop road, if you stop before you exit, you will hear the howl of the dog in the distance. The howl will gradually get closer and louder, until it seems to be right outside your vehicle. Many years ago, the statue of the dog was stolen. Visit the Reily Historical Society to see the only known photo of the dog on the tombstone.

Another legend in the cemetery involves another tombstone and also ends in vandalism. The Heard family stone had a life-sized stone statue of an angel holding his trumpet. A legend began that you could hear the angel blowing his trumpet at times in the cemetery. The statue has fallen victim to many years of damage from vandals. The wings are missing, and one hand is gone, as is the trumpet. It also looks like it was toppled and reset in the past.

The damaged angel standing over the Heard family graves was, sadly, vandalized over decades by thrill seekers. *Author's collection.*

Other stories involve the apparition of a boy wearing suspenders seen in the cemetery who just vanishes from sight. Likewise, some people have seen a strange fog near the cemetery, with sounds like voices coming from inside of it. Given the history of vandalism, maybe the voices in the cloud are there to keep an eye on things.

CHAPTER 9

GRIM REAPINGS

THE BLOODY GHOST OF THE FAIRGROUNDS

A ghost of a man is said to have been seen wandering around the Butler County Fairgrounds at night. The people who claim to have seen him say he was covered in blood. Many say it looked like it was from a head wound. Typically, he is seen behind the grandstands or walking out of the restroom. Some say he has a glowing aura. His clothing is never described.

In 1856, the Butler County Agricultural Society opened the fairgrounds. The fairgrounds have seen many fairs in their time. They have also seen death, including two incidents in 1943 when men were killed in different motorcycle races. In August 1960, a fifteen-year-old Middletown boy was killed when he was hit by the tire of a midget racer that flew over the fence. These fatalities and others could explain the ghost, but there are other possibilities dating to the Civil War.

Camp Hamilton opened in the Butler County Fairgrounds less than two weeks after the attack on Fort Sumter on April 12, 1861. William Miller, a local community leader, took charge of Camp Hamilton for its first three months, until he received a commission. Miller was on a scouting mission in September 1861 in West Virginia and, after a skirmish, climbed a tree searching for Confederates. A soldier from a Kentucky regiment, also scouting for Confederates, saw Miller in the distance, mistook him for the enemy and sent a killing shot. Miller was not the first Butler County casualty of the Civil War.

Grandstand at the Butler County Fair, 1950s. Photograph by Joseph A. Cella. *Lane Public Library, Joseph A. Cella Digital Photograph Collection.*

It was the morning of July 6, 1861, outside Buckhannon, Virginia. Near a bridge in control of the Confederates, Private John Falconer and his friend and fellow Hamiltonian Private Samuel R. John rose to charge. As they rose, they were met with a volley of gunfire. Falconer wrote in a letter to his father:

> *At the first volley, he was standing at my right side, his shoulder touching mine, and he was shot through the body. He called "John, John, I am killed, I am killed." I laid him on his side, saw his eyes turn glassy, his face grow pale and his lips blue and blood gush from his mouth.*

Sketch of soldiers in their tents in an army camp by Alfred R. Waud (1860s). This sight was probably similar to what was set up in the Butler County Fairgrounds. *Morgan Collection of Civil War drawings, Library of Congress.*

Private Falconer survived the war and became Captain Falconer, but during victory celebrations at Appomattox Court House, he was accidentally killed by a celebratory gunshot.

Outside of Chattanooga, Tennessee, on November 25, 1863, the men of Butler County and Ohio put up a valiant fight during the Battle of Missionary Ridge. The men charged up the slopes and breached the Confederate line that General Sherman called impregnable. Sergeant William Stokes reached the top of the ridge, and as he waved his hat in victory, an enemy bullet penetrated his skull. The casualties were high on both sides, with 753 men killed on the Union side and 361 Confederates killed. Twelve men were from Butler County.

There is no definite answer as to who the fairgrounds ghost may be: a fair accident victim or a lost soul that began his march toward death from Camp Hamilton.

THE HATCHET MAN

According to the local folklore, if you enter Hickory Flat Cemetery at night, you will be chased out by a murderer wielding a hatchet that lurks in the cemetery. Sometimes he is heard in the cemetery banging his hatchet on the mausoleum door, which also bears hatchet marks. Although, with no mausoleums in the graveyard, maybe the legend is referring to the church or shed. Legend also says the caretaker of the cemetery was killed by the man, but the true story is much worse.

As told in local history books, in the 1840s, a family of German immigrants lived in a cabin in the woods near Busenbark. Busenbark, a small train stop, was near where Edgewood High School is today. A mile west of this intersection lies Hickory Flat Cemetery, the location of our ghost story. When the farmer imbibed too much, he would become abusive to his family. After one such incident, a neighbor called the sheriff, and the farmer was taken to jail in Hamilton. While he was in jail, the family's cabin door was found hacked open by an axe with the bodies of the children inside. The wife was found hacked to death in the nearby woods. The sheriff assumed the imprisoned farmer did the dastardly deed, but how? The farmer was able to sneak out of the prison one night, travel from Hamilton to Busenbark

The Hatchet Man has been seen late at night in the Hickory Flat cemetery. *Author's collection.*

on the train, kill the family and return to the prison. He was found out by blood discovered on his clothes. He was tried, convicted and hanged. This story is partly true.

The story in the July 19, 1849 edition of the *Hamilton Intelligencer* had the headline: "Foul Murder in Butler County." The body of a woman, Sarah Yargus, was found murdered on the morning of July 14. Mrs. Yargus lived alone on the second floor of a house owned by John Good in St. Clair Township. Residing on the first floor were Frederick and Elizabeth Miller.

Mrs. Yargus lived alone because her husband was in custody at the Butler County Jail, and the children, John Jr., Commodore and Diana, did not live with them. John Yargus had been increasingly abusive to his wife since his return home from the Ohio State Penitentiary in 1846. Sarah filed a "peace warrant" against her abusive husband in April 1849.

When Yargus returned to an empty home on leaving the penitentiary, he demanded Sarah move back with him or he would kill her, so Sarah returned home. In April 1849, Commodore became worried about abuse toward his mother, even recalling his father saying, "What he intended to do, would be done yet." A few days before he was arrested on the peace warrant, John Yargus asked his neighbor John Johns if he had seen his wife or son Commodore. He accused them of stealing his dirk cane, a cane with a concealed dagger, and said he planned to get a pistol and kill them both. John Jr. said his father had threatened to kill them with his dagger previously. His father had also proclaimed, "I made this cane to do what I intended to do, even if it takes me twenty years!"

John Johns already had concerns about the safety of Sarah Yargus after previous exchanges with John Yargus. The previous winter, Johns was helping Yargus slaughter a pig for the winter, and he asked if a single pig would be enough for him and his wife. Yargus replied, "That hog will be as much as that old woman will ever need." He gave the same response when he later purchased flour.

On the evening of Friday, the thirteenth of July, 1849, Sarah Yargus was visited by her son Commodore. As he went to leave, his mother asked him to stay the night because tonight, for some reason, she was afraid. He told her that she was in no more danger; his father was in jail in Hamilton.

"Murder! Murder!" Those were the screams followed by a loud thump from the upstairs room that awakened Frederick and Elizabeth Miller. Miller jumped up to dress himself so he could check on his upstairs neighbor, Sarah Yargus. As he was doing so, he heard someone walking slowly down the stairs. Looking out the window, he saw a man in a dark coat and hat whom he immediately recognized: John Yargus. Miller did not go out of his room that night. He told his wife that if she wanted to check on Sarah, she could go herself; he was waiting until morning. Miller was afraid for his life because of Yargus, very afraid. He had provided sworn testimony during the peace warrant trial, claiming he heard Yargus threaten Sarah's life. Later, friends of Miller's alleged that he may have lied during his testimony. They said Miller felt bad about testifying against Yargus, especially since Sarah had become a less-than-pleasant neighbor. Miller told friends that his upstairs neighbor had become loud and quarrelsome and caused such a ruckus that his wife "couldn't raise her bread." Miller referred to Sarah Yargus as "the old witch" to his friends and tearfully said that if he'd had the five dollars for Yargus's bail, he would have posted it himself. He also insinuated that the reason he had to testify against Yargus was because if he didn't, his wife would have thrown him out.

That morning, he and his wife went upstairs. They saw blood on the entry and on the steps also a bloody handprint on the top of the outside gate. Miller didn't even make it all the way up the stairs. He stopped when he saw the legs of Sarah Yargus lying motionless on the floor in a pool of blood. Then Miller decided to go to Miltonville to fetch John Yargus Jr.

John Good, the owner of the house where Sarah Yargus lived, was the first to see the murder scene. He described the scene at the trial, as reported by the *Hamilton Intelligencer*:

> *I saw the body of Sarah Yargus…lying on the floor, her feet towards the door; her throat cut about 6 inches; her nose cut off, a bruise on her face, and there seemed to be a wound on the side of her head, near her ear. As the blood was running out of it. There was a brick broken in two on the floor, with hair matted in blood on the pieces; found the nose in the blood on the floor—it seemed to be cut with a sharp instrument.*

Good and Commodore both went to the jail and examined Yargus's clothing. Good stated he saw a stain on Yargus's shirt that looked like the stain on his own shirt after he laid out the body of Sarah Yargus. Commodore said he found bloodstains on his father's hat and his father's boots had new soles, which had a blood-like stain oozing from between the old sole and the new. Good also mentioned finding a hymn book outside the house a week after the murder, one he had given to John Yargus while he was in jail.

John Yargus, months after his wife pursued the peace warrant against him, had become a trusty under Sheriff Ferdinand VanDerveer. The morning of

Yargus was a trusty at the Butler County Jail, built in 1846. This photo is from the 1960s. Located across from the county courthouse, it remained in service until the new jail opened in 1971. *Lane Public Library, George C. Cummins "Remember When" Photograph Collection.*

the murder, Yargus was seen talking to and sharing some tobacco with the sheriff in front of the jail. He approached Stephen Kirk later that day and asked if he could provide two horses and a wagon to take him out to the country to pick up his furniture. Kirk said he wasn't able to that night, and Yargus said he'd do it himself and, while he was out there, he'd "sweep the platter." Around nine o'clock that night, Yargus was seen purchasing whiskey from Lohman's bar. Later, Richard Johnson saw Yargus in Caldwell's store and watched him purchase a candle. He was last seen that night by the tollgate keeper walking on the pike toward Trenton.

Yargus was charged with the murder of his wife on Saturday, July 14, 1849. The trial began on October 1, 1849. John Yargus submitted a plea of not guilty. Testimony was given by John Good, the Millers and others, including all three of Yargus's children. The trial lasted four days, and on October 4, John Yargus was found guilty of second-degree murder. He was sentenced to return to the Ohio State Penitentiary for life. It was a sentence he never served.

John Yargus was found dead in his cell the morning of October 11, his neck apparently slashed with a razor by his own hand. The *Hamilton Telegraph* on October 18, 1849, ran a story titled, "The Way of the Transgressor Is Hard." The article said Yargus was being sent to the Ohio State Penitentiary that same day and speculated the razor he used to kill himself was the same one he used on his wife.

The murder weapon was never mentioned in the news reports, aside from the brick Yargus used to smash his wife's head. John Good theorized during his testimony that she had suffered knife cuts. The wounds were described as a cut from ear to ear or cuts on both sides of the neck, severing the jugular but not perforating the esophagus. They were probably made with a straight razor, one that John Yargus did own. Why is he called the Hatchet Man and not the Razor Man? It was probably because of the story his daughter told during the murder trial. Diana stated that when they were younger, once, with the three children present and in the heat of anger, John stormed outside and came back carrying an axe and a trough. He said that the trough was to catch every bit of Sarah's blood when he slaughtered her with the hatchet. It was a terrifying and revealing look into the mind of a madman, one the public would probably not forget for a long time. Perhaps not coincidentally, his threat was prophetic. It was eerily similar to how he killed himself. In that early hour of October 11, John Yargus retrieved his trusty straight razor, and lying on the bed with his head and neck hanging over the edge, over a large bucket he had placed on the floor to catch his blood, he slit his own throat.

The murder was remembered and talked about by the people of Butler County for decades. In 1893, a journalist spent the night in the Butler County jail to write about the prison experience for the *Hamilton Evening Journal*. He was put in a cell for the night, "The same cell…in which forty years ago, 'Old Yargus' committed suicide by cutting his throat." The entire Yargus murder story was also retold in the February 11, 1904 *Butler County Democrat* column titled Exciting Events. For more than fifty years, the story did not go away, and neither did John Yargus.

The figure stood in the cemetery, a white face with two black holes for eyes staring out from under a black hat and black coat. The large, hulking shape just stared at the car as it slowly traveled along Wehr Road. The people in the car looked out and stared back, mouths agape, until one of them screamed, "It's the Hatchet Man!"

This incident occurred in 1992, as a young man and his two cousins went to the cemetery late one night. The ghost in the cemetery isn't the only phenomenon experienced by people near the cemetery. There were tales of an old barn nearby where the Hatchet Man supposedly hung the bodies. Another peculiar story was of a carload of people driving past whose car was assaulted by ears of corn flying out of a nearby cornfield. Even creepier were the tales of people in black robes standing in the road.

The names had been forgotten and the details changed considerably over the past 175 years. It has been a story I have wanted to uncover ever since my friend Jason Allen called me at two o'clock in the morning saying that he and his two cousins saw the Hatchet Man that night in 1992. It took me over thirty years to uncover all of the history behind this haunting.

EPILOGUE

A CAUTIONARY TALE

Many people are intrigued by their local mysterious legends and folklore and want to see for themselves and have their own experiences. Sadly, this leads to many sites being broken into and, many times, vandalized, like the grave markers in the Reily Cemetery. Sometimes, this can have horrible consequences beyond property damage.

On Sunday night, January 15, 1962, a group of teens were at a drive-in in Hamilton. While talking, some girls brought up some stories. The group of ten decided to visit a rumored haunted house on Herman Road, near Ross. The teens drove from Hamilton and pulled in front of the home. The dark, foreboding building looked like the quintessential haunted house. It was in disrepair, the yard unkempt, paint peeling; there were broken windows and no signs of life. The house was originally an 1812 log cabin, with additional structures added over the years.

The group, six girls and four boys, debated in front of the house about who would go in. One of the girls called John Langhorst a "chicken." That convinced the eighteen-year-old University of Cincinnati freshman that he had to be the one. So he approached the front door of the dilapidated domicile and gathered his courage to try the door. The old, rusted knob didn't turn. Someone yelled from behind him, "Put some muscle into it, John!" He stepped back and put his shoulder into the door; the door burst open; next, he saw a flash and an explosion. John felt burning pains in his neck. He fell onto a stack of firewood, then managed to stand up, and as he turned toward the door, there was another flash and explosion. John Langhorst staggered out of the house, the girls by the cars shrieked in terror and he fell to the ground, dead.

A short while earlier, Harry Demeret, eighty-two, was lying down in bed when he heard cars outside, followed by voices. Ever since someone broke into his home a few weeks before, he had been sleeping with his shotgun and trusty .44 Colt revolver under his pillow. The night before, he heard voices outside and thought the burglars had returned, but they left without trying to get in. When he heard the shattering of splintered wood, he jumped up and ran to the front of the house. A man had busted in his door, and Harry fired. The man staggered and screamed as Harry fired again. The man stumbled out of the house and fell in the yard, dead.

Harry Demeret was a solitary soul. He had lived in that house since 1924. He had a roof over his head, although the house had no gas, electricity, telephone or running water. Why pay for water when he could walk to a stream on his 184-acre property and get as many buckets of nice fresh water as he needed? A nephew who lived nearby would bring him food and check up on him. He walked everywhere, including a twenty-mile round trip to Hamilton to pay his taxes every year. Over the years, he decided he didn't even need all seven rooms in his two-story house. He had one room furnished to suit his needs and plenty of space to store his firewood out of the rain and snow, enough to last many seasons. He just wanted to live his quiet life. He was so reclusive that some of the neighbors believed the house was abandoned. Gradually, the old house built up a reputation of being haunted.

There were no charges filed against Mr. Demeret. The shooting was classified as "justifiable homicide," as Mr. Demeret had believed his life and property was in danger. A night of thrill seeking and trespassing ended a young man's life.

The paranormal is a fun way to learn history, and if you're lucky, to have your own experience, but breaking laws, especially destroying tombstones and breaking and entering, isn't the way to do it. It proves nothing, and you don't want to end up paying fines, getting put in jail or becoming the next John Langhorst.

BIBLIOGRAPHY

Ashworth, Sam. *A History of Sorg's Opera House*. Middletown, OH: Fool's Press, 1991.

Baker, Shirley, and Esther Benzing. *Indian Creek Pioneer Burial Ground and Church Restoration and Dedication*. Middletown, OH: RGI Public Relations, 1985.

Bartlow, Bert Surene. *Centennial History of Butler County, Ohio*, Indianapolis, Indiana: B.F. Bowen, 1905.

BCSO History. https://www.butlersheriff.org/about/bcso-history/.

Blount, Jim. *Butler County Biographies*. Hamilton, OH: Past/Present/Press, 2001.

———. *Butler County Place Names*. N.p., 2005.

———. *Butler County's Greatest Weather Disaster Flood March 1913*. Hamilton, OH: Past/Present/Press, 2002.

———. *A Century of Electric Generation in Hamilton, Ohio 1895–1995*. N.p., 1995.

———. *The Civil War and Butler County*. Hamilton, OH: Past/Present/Press, 1998.

———. *Fort Hamilton Diary: The St. Clair Campaign*. Hamilton, OH: Past/Present/Press, 1996.

———. *Greenwood Biographies A Hamilton Bicentennial Project of the Greenwood Cemetery Association 1848–1991*. Hamilton, OH: Greenwood Cemetery, 1991.

———. *Hamilton's Centennial in Retrospect: A 1991 Look at 1891 in Hamilton, Ohio and Observance of the City's 100th Anniversary*. Hamilton, OH: Hamilton Bicentennial Commission, 1991.

————. *Historical Vignettes About People, Places, & Events in Hamilton! And Butler County, Ohio Volume 1.* Hamilton, OH: Past/Present/Press, 1995.

————. *A History of Travel in Hamilton! And Butler County Ohio On the Road.* Hamilton, OH: Past/Present/Press, 1996.

————. *Little Chicago Volume 1, The Early Years, 1919–1927.* Hamilton, OH: Past/Present/Press, 1997.

————. *Little Chicago Volume 2, The Deadly Years, 1928–1942.* Hamilton, OH: Past/Present/Press, 1997.

————. *Railroads of Butler County.* Hamilton, OH: Past/Present/Press, 1999.

————. *The Road to Fort Hamilton.* Hamilton, OH: Journal-News and the Golden Triangle Association, 1976.

————. *Rossville: Hamilton's West Bank: Its People, Ghosts, Places Bridges & Businesses.* Hamilton, OH: Past/Present/Press, 1994.

Blount, Jim, George Crout and Dr. Phillip R. Shriver. *The 1900s: 100 Years in the History of Butler County, Ohio.* Hamilton, OH: Past/Present/Press, 2000.

The Butler County Atlas and Pictorial Review 1914. Hamilton, OH: Republican Publishing, 1914.

Butler County Historical Society. https://www.bchistoricalsociety.com.

Casper, Teri, and Dan Smith. *Ghosts of Cincinnati.* Charleston, SC: The History Press, 2009.

The County of Butler, Ohio: An Imperial Atlas and Art Folio. Richmond, IN: Rerick Brothers, Topographers and Publishers, 1895.

Crane, John. *1855 Butler County Map.* N.p., 1855.

Crout, George. *Bicentennial Briefs.* N.p., 1991.

Eblin, Jennifer. *Haunted Miami Valley.* Charleston, SC: The History Press, 2010.

Eckert, Allan W. *That Dark and Bloody River: Chronicles of the Ohio River Valley.* New York: Bantam, 1995.

————. *The Frontiersman: A Narrative.* Ashland, KY: Jesse Stuart Foundation, 2001.

Everts, L.H. *Combination Atlas Map of Butler County Ohio, 1875.* Philadelphia: Hunter Publishing, 1875.

Greater Hamilton CVB. *Walking Tours of Historic Hamilton, Ohio.* Hamilton, OH: Hamilton Graphics, n.d.

Heider, Alta Harvey. *Hamilton in the Making.* Oxford, OH: Mississippi Valley Press, 1941.

Horwitz, Lester V. *The Longest Raid of the Civil War.* Cincinnati, OH: Farmcourt Publishing, 1999.

Hunter, Bob. *Road to Wapatomica.* Columbus, OH: Culloden Books, 2020.

Hurt, R. Douglas. *The Ohio Frontier.* Bloomington: Indiana University Press, 1996.

Johannesen, Eric. *Ohio College Architecture before 1870.* Columbus: Ohio Historical Society, 1969.

Lake, D.J. *Butler County Map, 1868.* Philadelphia: C.O. Titus, 1868.

Laven, Karen. *Cincinnati Ghosts.* Atglen, PA: Schiffer Publishing, 2008.

MacLean, John Patterson. *The Mound Builders.* Cincinnati, OH: Robert Clarke, 1879.

Map Makers Atlas and Plat Book of Butler County, Ohio, 1930: Compiled from Surveys and the Public Records of Butler County, Ohio. Rockford, IL: Thrift Press, 1930.

Martin, Matthew. "Monroe Ohio Historical Museum—1910 House." Clio: Your Guide to History, July 12, 2015. https://www.theclio.com/entry/16315.

McAlester, Virginia Savage. *A Field Guide to American Houses.* New York: Alfred A. Knopf 2013.

McBride, James. *1836 Butler County, Ohio Township Maps.* N.p., 1836.

McCartt, Marcia. *Monroe.* Images of America series. Charleston, SC: Arcadia Publishing, 2009.

McClung, David Waddle. *The Centennial Anniversary of the City of Hamilton, Ohio, September 17–19, 1891.* Hamilton, OH: Lawrence Printing and Publishing, 1892.

Mills, William C. *Archeological Atlas of Ohio.* Columbus, OH: Ohio State Archaeological and Historical Society, 1914.

Morris, Jeff, and Michael Morris. *Cincinnati Haunted Handbook.* Cincinnati, OH: Clerisy Press 2010.

National Park Service. U.S. Civil War Soldiers, 1861–1865 [database online]. Provo, UT: Ancestry.com, 2007.

Ohio Sandborn Maps. https://sanborn.ohioweblibrary.org/.

Ohio State Archaeological and Historical Society. *The Ohio Guide, Compiled by Workers of the Writers of the Work Projects Administration in the State of Ohio.* New York: Oxford University Press, 1946.

O'Neill, Shi. *Haunted Hamilton, Ohio.* Charleston, SC: The History Press, 2021.

Page, Doris L. *Miltonville's Story.* Middletown, OH: Letter Perfect, 1986.

———. *Where Was Busenbark?* Middletown, OH: Letter Perfect, 1991.

Roberts, Matt. "Reily's Pizza." *Cincinnati Ghosts* (blog). December 29, 2016. https://cincinnatighosts.wordpress.com/2016/12/29/reilys-pizza/.

Scamyhorn, Richard, and John Steinle. *Stockades in the Wilderness.* St. Martin, OH: Commonwealth Book Company, 2020.

Schmidt Cahill, Lora, and David L. Mowery. *Morgan's Raid across Ohio.*

Columbus: Ohio Historical Society, 2013.

Sesqui-Centennial Monroe 1817–1967. City of Monroe, 1967.

Squier, Ephraim George, and Edwin Hamilton Davis. *Ancient Monuments of the Mississippi Valley.* Washington, D.C.: Smithsonian Institution, 1848.

"State of Ohio vs. John Yargus." *Common Pleas Journal* 20: 188. 1849 County Records Center and Archives, Hamilton, OH.

Stille, Samuel Harden. *Ohio Builds a Nation.* Lower Salem, OH: Arlendale Bookhouse, n.d.

Symmes, John Cleves, and James McBride. *Symmes's Theory of Concentric Spheres.* Cincinnati, OH: Morgan, Lodge and Fisher, 1826.

Triplett, Boone. *Canals of Ohio: A History and Tour Guide.* Wadsworth, OH: Silver Sassafras Publications, 2011.

Walking Tour of Oxford's University Historic District. Oxford, OH: Smith Library of Regional History, 2008.

Walking Tour of Oxford's Uptown Historic District. Oxford, OH: Smith Library of Regional History, 2017.

Walking Tour of Oxford's Western College for Women Historic District. Oxford, OH: Smith Library of Regional History, 2014.

Ware, Jane. *Building Ohio: A Traveler's Guide to Ohio's Rural Architecture.* Wilmington, OH: Orange Frazier Press, 2002.

Wilcox Frank N. *Ohio Indian Trails.* Cleveland, OH: Gates Press, 1934.

Williams, Gary S. *The Forts of Ohio: A Guide to Military Stockades.* Caldwell, OH: Buckeye Book Press, 2003.

Woodward, Susan L., and Jerry N. McDonald. *Indian Mounds of the Middle Ohio Valley.* Saline, MI: McDonald and Woodward Publishing, 2001.

Woodyard, Chris. *The Face in the Window.* Beavercreek, OH: Kestrel Publications, 2013.

———. *Haunted Ohio.* Beavercreek, OH: Kestrel Publications, 1991.

———. *Haunted Ohio IV.* Beavercreek, OH: Kestrel Publications, 1997.

———. *Haunted Ohio III.* Beavercreek, OH: Kestrel Publications, 1994.

———. *Haunted Ohio II.* Beavercreek, OH: Kestrel Publications, 1992.

———. *The Headless Horror Tales.* Beavercreek, OH: Kestrel Publications, 2013.

———. *Spooky Ohio: 13 Traditional Tales.* Beavercreek, OH: Kestrel Publications, 1995.

Zimmerman, Fritz. *The Nephilim Chronicles: A Travel Guide to Ancient Ruins in the Ohio Valley.* N.p., 2010.

About the Author

D aniel D. Schneider is an avid traveler and always eager to learn. Born and raised in Hamilton, Daniel spent several decades in the Columbus, Ohio area, although he was back in Hamilton very frequently. He moved back in 2019. A registered landscape architect and 3D designer, Daniel started his own design firm in 2021 and named it Hollow Earth Creative after the Symmes Hollow Earth theory and nearby Hollow Earth monument. While in Columbus, Daniel researched, wrote and conducted many haunted tours for the Columbus Landmarks Foundation and also for the League of Women Voters Haunted Tours in Chillicothe, Ohio.

Daniel is a member of many local historical groups and is currently a board member for Historic Hamilton and CHAPS (Citizens for Historic and Preservation Services), Butler County's historic preservation group. He also serves on the City of Hamilton's Architectural Design Review Board and is on the city's 17 Strong Neighborhood Communications Committee. Daniel has traveled the United States and Europe seeking out the historical, haunted and strange.

The author with a Krampus in Salzburg, Austria. *Author's collection.*

FREE eBOOK OFFER

Scan the QR code below, enter your e-mail address and get our original Haunted America compilation eBook delivered straight to your inbox for free.

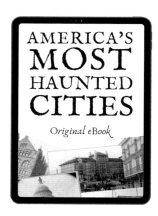

ABOUT THE BOOK

Every city, town, parish, community and school has their own paranormal history. Whether they are spirits caught in the Bardo, ancestors checking on their descendants, restless souls sending a message or simply spectral troublemakers, ghosts have been part of the human tradition from the beginning of time.

In this book, we feature a collection of stories from five of America's most haunted cities: Baltimore, Chicago, Galveston, New Orleans and Washington, D.C.

SCAN TO GET
AMERICA'S MOST HAUNTED CITIES

Having trouble scanning? Go to:
biz.arcadiapublishing.com/americas-most-haunted-cities